[redacted]

The CHIAPAS Rebellion

by
Philip L. Russell

MEXICO RESOURCE CENTER
Box 7547 • Austin, Texas 78713

Printed in the United States of America

Library of Congress Cataloging in Publication Data: 94-73330

ISBN: 0-9639223-1-9

Front-cover photo by Eloy Valtierra (Cuartoscuro) reproduced with permission. Other photos reproduced with permission are by Paulina Hermosillo (Retrato Hablado), Duncan Earle (Center for Housing and Urban Development, Texas A&M University), and Eduardo Vera (Austin Committee in Solidarity with Chiapas and Mexico).

Front map reproduced from *A Rich Land, A Poor People: Politics and Society in Modern Chiapas* with permission of Thomas Benjamin. Map on p. 21 reproduced with permission of *Cultural Survival Quarterly*. Map on p. 126 reproduced with permission of the *New York Times*.

Copy editing by Shelly Ogle

TABLE OF CONTENTS

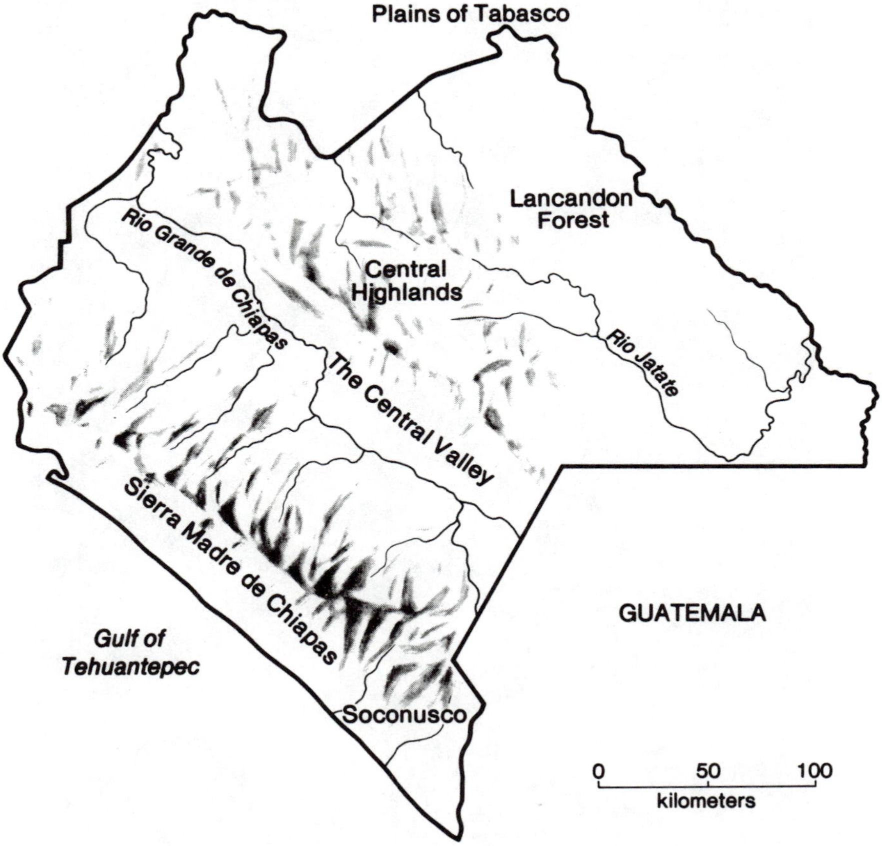

The Topography of the
State of Chiapas

Marcos *Paulina Hermosillo*

Chapter 1: Causes

> The Zapatistas have pulled back the curtain that covered up the other Mexico. It is not the Mexico of eager entrepreneurs lined up to open Pizza Hut franchises or consumers eager to shop at Wal-Mart, but rather the Mexico of malnourished children, illiteracy, landlessness, poor roads, lack of health clinics, and life as a permanent struggle.
>
> — Lynn Stephen, 1994[1]

The Chiapas rebellion, which broke out on 1 January 1994, was widely portrayed as a protest against the North American Free Trade Agreement (NAFTA), which went into effect that day. The revolt, however, arose from a combination of long-standing grievances.

Underlying the uprising is the status of Indians, who constitute 30 percent of Chiapas' population.[2] Unlike most areas in Mexico, Chiapas has seen little biological race mixing (known as *mestizaje*). Instead, for centuries, Indians and non-Indians have occupied separate domains.[3]

Ethnic conflict dates back to the Spanish conquest. Indians rebelled against Spanish domination in 1532 and 1534. The better armed Spaniards, however, soon defeated the rebels. This rebellion was only the first in a cyclical process of grievance accumulation, rebellion, suppression, and then the accumulation of more grievances.[4]

Indians in Chiapas rebelled again in 1712 after a young Indian woman, María de la Candelaria, reported that the Virgin Mary had appeared to her and told her to build a chapel in her honor. A cult soon sprang up to honor the Virgin. Its followers declared, "*Ya no hay Dios ni Rey* (Neither God nor the King exist any longer)." This defiant cry reflected the cult members' rejection of both Spanish political control and the Catholic-defined notion of the deity.

Spanish authorities attempted to suppress the cult, threatening to punish its leaders and burn the chapel constructed to honor the Virgin. This led to rebellion. The rebels organized their own priesthood and political system and raised an army of 5,000 whose soldiers referred to themselves as "Soldiers of the Virgin." As historian Enrique Florescano noted, "The Soldiers of the Virgin went into combat against the Spanish convinced that they were protected by supernatural forces." For three months, Indians sacked Catholic churches and Spanish estates, killing Spanish and mestizo settlers, as well as five Dominican curates. Colonial authorities were only able to suppress the rebellion after troops arrived from Guatemala, of which Chiapas was then a part.[5]

The threat of losing land led to another uprising in 1867. Anthropologist Ricardo Pozas comments on this rebellion:

> The real causes of the rebellion were the economic misery in which the Indians lived and the danger reform posed for Indian communal land. All a claimant had to do to obtain legal title to Indian lands was to give notice that they were in fact communally held.[6]

The rebels rejected Mexican government authority. They banned the use of money, allowing only barter. The rebels declared: "Non-Indians have the money, and we have the produce. Let the non-Indians eat their money, and we'll eat our produce."[7]

A "caste war" soon broke out. More than 4,000 Indians besieged the state capital of San Cristóbal in early 1869. Gov. José Pantaleón Domínguez mobilized the state militia, which was finally able to defeat the ill-prepared Indian force.[8]

Change in the status of Indians has come slowly. As recently as the 1950s, Indians trekked to San Cristóbal, carrying their merchandise on their backs. They were forbidden to enter the city and were forced to sell to intermediaries, who then resold the merchandise in San Cristóbal for a quick profit. Today, trucks carry goods to market on roads. However, Indian producers still sell their goods to non-Indian truck owners, who pay Indians only a small portion of the product's final sale price.[9]

Unfortunately, non-Indians' attitudes toward Indians have not changed as rapidly as the economic ties. In 1971, a sign in the Ocosingo Lion's Club, declared:

> La Ley del Monte ordena que
> al indio y al zanate...
> se le mate...
>
> The law of the jungle says
> you kill
> Indians and grackles.[10]

Patrocinio González Garrido, governor of Chiapas between 1988 and 1993, referred to Indians as the FBI (*fuerza bruta indígena*—brute Indian force).[11]

In his August 1993 pastoral letter, Samuel Ruiz, bishop of San Cristóbal, commented on the lot of the Indian today:

> Indigenous people are humiliated and tricked. They are forced to vote for the PRI. Officials are imposed on them against their will. They are not permitted to organize. There is repression in both the city and the countryside. The police and the army control them. Their authorities are corrupt. There is illiteracy, poor schooling, and a lack of electricity, drinking water, and sanitation facilities. There are also irresponsible teachers and excessive school fees. The only health services they receive are birth control and abortion.[12]

Subcommander Marcos, the high-profile rebel spokesman, said that San Cristóbal deserved to be attacked on New Year's Day because its residents were particularly cruel to Indians. However, he emphasized that the Indians restrained themselves and did not exact vengeance there for the "numerous humiliations which they suffer daily."[13]

A major, long-standing complaint of the Indian community is the control of land by non-Indians. In other areas of Mexico, the Mexican Revolution reduced the social tension created by the concentration of land ownership. Early in this century, the need for reform in Chiapas was even more pressing, since the elite was determined not only to maintain its land holdings but to also continue imposing debt servitude on its labor force.[14]

Rather than accepting reform, the elite managed to avoid most of the changes promised by the Revolution. As historian Thomas Benjamin notes, "The fuel of Mexico's agrarian revolution, the landless and exploited peasantry, in Chiapas and the southern regions generally was too divided, controlled, and isolated to burn down the old order."[15]

Between 1914 and 1920, low-land ranchers and estate owners in Chiapas organized a successful counter-revolution whose participants were known as *mapaches.* Besides wanting to retain control of land and labor, the mapaches resented the revolutionaries' anticlericalism. They also resented the state's being placed under the control of military officers sent from outside Chiapas.[16]

In 1919, revolutionary general Álvaro Obregón, who was in the process of overthrowing fellow revolutionary Venustiano Carranza, agreed to support the mapaches if they would support his coup.[17] The offer was accepted. Thus, mapache leader Tiburcio Fernández Ruiz became governor of Chiapas after Carranza was overthrown. Chiapan historian José Casahonda Castillo describes Fernández Ruiz, who became governor in 1920:

> He was a cattleman and as such had their characteristic virtues and defects. He was a staunch conservative and opposed any change in the social order into which he was born. He loved the land passionately. He opposed land reform and kept his land until his death, the same land that his parents and his grandparents had cherished before him. He was the backbone, the core, the true leader of the mapache movement. There was no questioning his authority. Thanks to him and his men, the social reforms in Chiapas were postponed.[18]

As governor, Fernández Ruiz decreed that individual private landowners could maintain estates as large as 8,000 hectares (31 square miles). Even that limit was not enforced. In 1930, 29 estates in Chiapas were larger than 10,000 hectares.[19]

During the presidency of Lázaro Cárdenas (1934-40), central-government intervention in Chiapas increased. Cárdenas even showed his concern for Chiapas by visiting in 1940, the first Mexican president to do so. It took several days for Cárdenas to reach the state—traveling by car, steamboat, train, and, finally, horse. Only in 1946 was the highway to San Cristóbal finally inaugurated.[20]

During the Cárdenas administration, the federal Department of Indigenous Affairs declared that "conditions of virtual slavery exist in Chiapas." Under Cárdenas, leadership positions at the state level were opened to indigenous people.

However, just as the lofty edicts of the Spanish Crown were often ignored in Mexico during the colonial period, Cárdenas' zeal for land reform was largely ignored in Chiapas. Despite the transfer of 252,882 hectares to the *ejido* sector between 1933 and 1940, large estates survived virtually intact. In 1930, properties larger than 5,000 hectares constituted 29 percent of private land in Chiapas. By the end of the decade, they still accounted for 27 percent.[21]

Even though land was transferred to Indians at this time, social problems persisted. Much of the land transferred was of poor quality. The result was a labor force tied to the land and forced to supplement its income by working on coffee plantations. With few exceptions, the land distributed had been unused forest, not productive private holdings. Enrique Brawn was one of the few landowners to lose substantial amounts of cultivated land in the redistribution. The taking of 3,872.6 hectares of his land during the Cárdenas administration did not reflect a concern for social justice. Rather, it reflected his failure to bribe officials not to take the land.[22]

After 1950, when settlement began in eastern Chiapas, land reform was also implemented there. More than 1.3 million hectares were transferred into the ejido sector in the municipalities of Ocosingo, Altamirano, and Las Margaritas. Despite this massive transfer of land, rural problems remained unresolved. In many cases, they worsened.

Ranchers were generally successful in ensuring that only poor-quality land was transferred to the communally held farms known as ejidos. They continued to dominate the region's economy, since they controlled the best pasture lands and most of the cattle and capital.[23] In some cases, owners retained holdings far in excess of the legal limits by registering their holdings in the names of front-men and relatives.[24]

Often, the process of land reform literally dragged out for decades. During this time, ranchers maintained use of the land while claimants were forced to spend large sums in their attempts to acquire the land they were legally entitled to. Retaliation from ranchers was common. For example, in 1940, the ejido Belisario Domínguez, in the municipality of Altamirano, was granted 1,568 hectares of land. It was five years later before the claimants actually received any land—312 hectares. In 1959, an additional 816 hectares of land were finally transferred to the ejido. By then, the remaining 440 hectares of the original grant had been transferred to others.[25]

Rather than processing claims of those soliciting land, authorities simply let them pile up for decades. As a result, almost 30 percent of Mexico's outstanding land claims (*rezago agrario*) are in Chiapas. Some 85,000 Chiapan peasants have 2,847 of such outstanding claims.[26]

Land affairs are fraught with official abuse. Peasant groups allied with the PRI are pitted against independent groups by favoring the former's land claims.[27] Overall, as author Jorge Castañeda notes, while in fact some land was being distributed, "the local authorities and the army worked with the cattle grazers in dispossessing the Indians of their communal lands."[28]

Even if all Chiapas' land problems had been resolved during the Cárdenas administration (and, of course, they weren't), that

Women in Las Margaritas *Paulina Hermosillo*

accomplishment would have been erased by subsequent population increase. Between 1940 and 1990, the population of the state increased from 679,885 to 3,210,496.[29] Between 1980 and 1990, it grew at 4.51 percent per year, more than double the national rate of 2.02 percent.[30]

There are several reasons for this rapid population growth. The birth rate in Chiapas is high, reflecting the worldwide pattern of high birth rates among women who have few educational and job opportunities outside of the home.

Only 12 percent of women in Chiapas are in the work force. In the highlands, Indian women care for an average of five children, plus a husband and other relatives. They spend an average of five hours a day just to mill *nixtamal* and make tortillas by hand. In addition, they must often walk long distances to obtain water and firewood, and then haul it home. In Altamirano, 93 percent of homes use firewood for cooking. In Ocosingo, 89 percent use firewood, and in Las Margaritas, 92 percent do.[31]

Columnist Dolores Cordero commented on the lot of Indian women:

> What childhood? At the age of six or seven years they are carrying a brother along, just like their mothers did. What adolescence? At the age of 11, 12, or 13 years, they are pregnant by the men who take them. What youth? From then on, there are births, which if they don't kill them, destroy them. From then on, always, they only obey. They are kept in second, or third, fourth, fifth, or tenth place, without laughing, without saying anything. They barely eat, they barely speak, they hardly smile, they're working.[32]

The population of the highlands almost tripled between 1950 and 1990, despite massive out-migration. In Chamula, the most crowded municipality, there were 269 people per square kilometer in 1950. By 1990, the density had reached 382.[33]

Beginning in the 1950s, a stream of indigenous people from the highlands began following lumber roads into the sparsely inhabited eastern lowlands. Residents of the highlands were encouraged to resettle in eastern Chiapas, since, as anthropologist Luis Hernández Navarro notes, "rather than touch the interests of the great landowners from the north and center of the state, the land petitioners were sent off on an adventure to colonize the forest."[34]

Beginning in the 1970s, non-Indians from other states also began to stream into eastern Chiapas. The national government encouraged them to do so to relieve land pressure in the other states.

Guatemalans who entered Mexico illegally further added to the population of the eastern lowlands. Cattle ranchers preferred hiring them, since they were willing to work for as little as 33 cents a day.[35] Due to their illegality, the Guatemalans did not assert their labor rights. The number of them working illegally in Chiapas reached an estimated 100,000.[36] During the 1980s, an additional 80,000 Guatemalans crossed into Chiapas fleeing the violence inflicted on indigenous people by the Guatemalan military.[37]

As a result of these factors, there has been explosive population growth in eastern Chiapas. In 1960, the 5,000 inhabitants of the area were largely members of the Chol and Lacandón indigenous groups. The population of the area is now 300,000.[38] Settlement in eastern Chiapas has been so pervasive that much of the forest cover has been removed. In neighboring Guatemala, the forest cover is relatively intact. As a result, due to the difference in shading, the countries' boundary is clearly visible from outer space.[39]

The newly emerged society in eastern Chiapas lacks the traditional top-down relations between citizens and government agencies—such as the PRI, the National Peasant Confederation (CNC), and the National Indigenous Institute (INI)—which serve to maintain social control in the highlands.[40] Adding to Chiapas' misery was the exhaustion of the supply of new land to colonize. This shut off an escape valve for the landless.[41]

In Chiapas, resolution of pressing social issues has not been possible through the democratic process. Election statistics in Chiapas are even more suspect than in Mexico as a whole. In the 1988 presidential elections, the percentage of people voting for the PRI in the state of Chiapas, according to official statistics, was 39 percent above the nationwide average. The 88.8 percent vote reported for the PRI was certainly not grateful citizens rewarding the incumbents for serving their interests. The highest percentage of registered voters reportedly casting votes for the PRI was in rural areas, where there were the lowest rates of literacy and few opposition poll watchers. In contrast, in Tuxtla Gutiérrez, the state capital, only 20.7 percent voted for the PRI.[42]

In the 1991 congressional elections, the reported percentage favoring the PRI in Chiapas was 76.3 percent, second nationwide only to nearby Campeche. In Oxchuc, the PRI obtained not 99.9 percent of the 11,073 votes cast, but 100 percent. That year, Chiapas was the Mexican state which reported the most municipalities casting every single vote for the PRI. Very high registration rates facilitated support for the PRI. In San Juan Cancuc, registration totaled 102 percent of its citizens.[43]

Subcommander Marcos commented on one of the reasons the PRI obtained such high percentages: "Polling stations were never set up in the highlands nor in the forest area. We found out that in the municipal seats people simply marked the ballots. Later you learned that the PRI had won with 90 or 100 percent."[44]

In 1991, the opposition Party of the Democratic Revolution (PRD) claimed it had won mayoral elections in Ocosingo and Las Margaritas (two municipalities later occupied by the rebels). Nevertheless, Gov. González Garrido awarded these mayoralties to the PRI candidates and jailed 153 PRD supporters.[45] The only recognized opposition victory was in Huixtán, where the PAN candidate won. Rather than reflecting even a minimal commitment to democracy, this reflected local bosses' having withdrawn support for the PRI candidate, since they felt he did not support them enough.[46]

In Chiapas, many municipalities, such as Huixtán, are under the control of local bosses known as *caciques*. They control affairs at the municipal level, and are maintained in power by the state political apparatus, as long as they deliver votes and keep the peace. Caciques, especially in the highlands, often control commerce, including the sale of soft drinks, flowers, candles, fireworks, and distilled spirits. These last two items are consumed in large quantities at festivals, which are an integral part of Indian life. To facilitate control, caciques organize their own armed protection forces.[47]

The expulsion of residents from Indian communities by caciques is a serious social problem in Chiapas in that it uproots thousands. Often, traditional Catholic caciques expel residents who have become Protestants. Such converts reduce spending on religious festivals, thus cutting into the caciques' economic base. Roughly 25,000 have been expelled from their communities in the past 20 years. Those challenging expulsion are frequently beaten or murdered.[48]

Another characteristic of Chiapan politics is the landed elite's holding of top political office itself, rather than trying to manipulate the political process to achieve the election of sympathetic office holders. As columnist Octavio Rodríguez Araujo notes, "Chiapas, rather than being a Mexican state, has remained as property of cattlemen, *hacendados*, politicians, and agro-exporters."[49]

The elite has successfully used its control of the political process to further its economic interests. As Benjamin notes, "My investigation of the history of Chiapas since Independence has brought me repeatedly to an understanding of the great importance of government as the essential shaping force of wealth and poverty in the region."[50]

The elite also tailored the legal system to serve its interests. Articles 129-35 of the state penal code provided prison terms of from two to four years for those who participate in unarmed mass protest, declaring them to be "threats to the public order." Using these provisions, the government "legally" suppressed protest.[51] The penal code also criminalized attacks on "historical, national, and state values" and made it illegal for anyone to "in any way or by any means invite a rebellion."[52] Chiapan Nicolás Gómez Chávez lamented: "When we try to organize and fight back, they call us agitators and throw us in jail. Who can we complain to? The cattle ranchers are the mayors, the judges, and the PRI officials. We have no place to turn."[53]

The experience of Joel Padrón, who served as village priest in Simojovel for years, provides an example of how the penal code was used. Padrón was arrested in 1991 and taken to Cerro Hueco prison in Tuxtla Gutiérrez. He was charged with 10 infractions of the code, including conspiracy. In exchange for Padrón's release, the government demanded five concessions. They were: 1) five specified parcels of land be vacated by squatters, 2) the Church formally condemn the taking of land by peasants, 3) the Church declare there are no violations of human rights in Chiapas, 4) lay teachers known as catechists cease inciting the taking of land by peasants, and 5) Padrón immediately leave the state after his release. Bishop Ruiz responded to these demands by commenting, "Either Joel will rot in jail for the rest of his life as an innocent man or he will be released *absolutely unconditionally*."[54]

Padrón obviously enjoyed support from his parishioners. Twelve thousand of them descended on Tuxtla Gutiérrez to demand his release.[55] Finally, after 49 days of incarceration, he was released unconditionally. His arrest led him to comment, "The police are not there to maintain social order, but to terrorize poor people."[56]

Taking advantage of their control of the political process, "estate owners, ranchers, and loggers organized their own paramilitary forces that acted with impunity against the campesinos."[57] These abuses date back for decades. Between 1965 and 1985, 25 Tzotzil Indian residents of Venustiano Carranza were killed as a result of conflict over 3,000 hectares of prime land. The land had been granted to them by presidential decree in 1965, but it remained occupied by ranchers and defended by hired gunmen.[58]

Governors have typically been landowners and have used security forces to protect the interests of large landholders. As an army general in 1980, Absalón Castellanos Domínguez, whose family has 14 estates totaling 20,000 hectares, ordered his troops to attack Indian villages.[59] He is the great-grandnephew of the governor who had suppressed the 1868 rebellion. Castellanos Domínguez was subsequently selected as governor of Chiapas. During his term, by one count, there were 153 political murders in the state, and 327 peasants disappeared. Many others were jailed and tortured.[60]

Patrocinio González Garrido succeeded Castellanos Domínguez as governor of Chiapas. He is a member of another elite family, and his father had served as governor of the state. His uncle, Tomás Garrido Canabal served as governor of neighboring Tabasco and was immortalized for his religious persecution in Graham Greene's novel *The Power and the Glory.*[61] Human-rights abuses continued unabated after González Garrido took office. In 1989, landowners' gunmen killed 12 peasants in the process of driving off those claiming land in Pijijiapan. The next year, police and landowners' gunmen drove off more than 100 families claiming land in Paso Achiote, Emiliano Zapata, and Unión y Progreso.[62] The assistant director of the newspaper *Diario de Chiapas* noted: "Terror was only a pretext to build an economic empire. Using terror, and under the guise of respect for the law, Don Patrocinio accumulated his inexplicable wealth."[63]

Despite such human-rights abuses and the conspicuous irregularities in the 1991 elections, González Garrido was promoted to the position of Interior Minster early in 1993. This put him directly in charge of national security forces and of organizing the 1994 presidential elections. His promotion shows that official abuse in Mexico is not only tolerated at the national level, but is rewarded.

Human-rights abuses continued unabated after the departure of González Garrido. In June 1993, Amnesty International reported that 1,000 members of state security forces, accompanied by local landlords, attacked the communities of Chalán del Carmen, Río Florido, Nuevo Sacrificio, Edén del Carmen, and El Carrizal.[64] A report by the Miguel Agustín Pro Human Rights Center summarized the 1993 human rights situation:

> The state of Chiapas is, as it was in 1992, the state with the most violations of rights of individuals and organizations. Most acts of aggression were committed against the Tzeltal and Tzotzil, as well as against mestizo peasants. The sector most affected was the Indian peasant. The most frequent violations were assaults and injuries, followed by arbitrary arrest, threats, torture, and murder.[65]

The underlying cause of social unrest in Chiapas is not that the state has somehow been "forgotten." Rather, it is the way in which Chiapas has been inserted into national and international markets. As Bishop Ruiz commented, "I oppose the neo-liberal modernization of the economy, not as a political gesture, but because the capitalist, global economy is dehumanizing—especially to the Indians."[66]

Chiapas is not inherently a poor state. Its hydroelectric stations produce 55 to 60 percent of Mexico's electricity, and its wells produce 21 percent of Mexico's oil and 47 percent of its natural gas. In addition, it yields more than half of Mexico's coffee crop, of which 68 percent is exported.[67] Other major sources of wealth are corn, timber, and cattle.

In Chiapas, there has traditionally existed an enormous gulf between landowner and worker. In the nineteenth century, the landed elite began coffee production in coastal areas of the state. Its members relied on the seasonal migration of indigenous people from the highlands to these plantations to provide labor for harvests.[68]

In the 1960s and 1970s, land barons and politicians encouraged Indians from the highlands to become sharecroppers as logging roads were opened in eastern Chiapas. These sharecroppers were forced to live in lean-tos to prevent them from establishing legal residency and claiming land under the land reform law. Land, which was cleared by the sharecroppers, would often be appropriated for raising cattle,

San Juan Chamula *Paulina Hermosillo*

forcing the sharecroppers to move on and clear additional land. In other cases, land was simply abandoned as it soon lost its fertility. This occurs quite rapidly, since heat kills microorganisms in soil exposed to direct sunlight. Also, in areas of high rainfall, nutrients are leached out of exposed soil.[69]

With the devaluation of the peso in 1976 and 1977, the domestic price of corn fell dramatically, depriving the corn produced by sharecroppers of much of its market value. This led landowners to accelerate the shift of land from sharecropping to cattle raising.[70] Employment opportunities thus decreased, since cattle ranching only requires about 1 percent as many people per hectare as farming.[71] Between 1982 and 1987, with government support, meat production increased by more than 400 percent.[72]

During the 1970s and into the 1980s, jobs created by government projects provided an alternative to small-scale peasant agriculture in the state. Two massive hydroelectric dams were built on the Grijalva River. Development of oil reserves also required extensive road building and stimulated commercial activity, thus employing many Chiapans in the state and in neighboring Tabasco. However, after the plunge in oil prices in 1982, such government-stimulated employment opportunities vanished. There were, in fact, fewer jobs than before since the reservoirs created by the dams flooded more than 200,000 hectares of land, thus eliminating agricultural jobs.[73]

Following this decrease in government investment, there was a sharp decrease in government intervention in the agriculture sector. This move, begun under President Miguel de la Madrid, left small producers without crop insurance, credit, fertilizer subsidies, or marketing facilities. This neglect of agriculture was typical of newly oil-rich nations, which assume that they can always use oil revenues to import food, rather than investing in food self-sufficiency.[74] Later, decreased support for agriculture reflected drastic cuts in government spending in an effort to balance the budget.

Government withdrawal from supporting coffee production had a major impact on Chiapas. In the late 1980s, the government vigorously promoted the widespread planting of coffee bushes and promised small producers credit, technical advice, and marketing assistance through an agency known as the Mexican Coffee Institute (INMECAFE). In 1989, as part of President Salinas' budget balancing, INMECAFE withdrew from purchasing and marketing coffee and reduced technical assistance. This organization was completely disbanded in 1993.[75] Also, following the 1989 failure of the International Coffee Organization to agree on production quotas, international coffee prices fell by 50 percent. The over-valued Mexican peso places coffee producers at a further disadvantage. In addition, wage-labor opportunities declined as growers with large coffee plantations reduced their work forces. Finally, 91 percent of Chiapas' 73,742 coffee producers occupy less than five hectares. These small producers have little access to credit and are at the mercy of commercial intermediaries known as *coyotes*. Small producers suffered an estimated 70 percent drop in income between 1989 and 1993.[76]

Cattle raising now ranks second behind coffee as the region's most important commercial activity. Expansion of the area devoted to raising cattle resulted in expulsion of the previous occupants of the land, closed off wage-labor opportunities for highland residents, and led to violent conflict over land.[77] In 1980, the latest date for which data is available, slightly more than 6,000 cattle-raising families in Chiapas held more than 3 million hectares, almost half of all land held by rural Chiapans.[78]

The price Chiapans received for prime beef plummeted from 76.5 cents a pound in 1992 to 54 cents a pound in 1994, hurting both large estate owners and many small producers. Cattlemen attributed this decline to imports from the United States capturing the beef market in central Mexico, a market formerly supplied from Chiapas.[79]

Corn producers also suffered. Beginning in 1987, the cost of inputs rose faster than corn prices, squeezing the producer.[80] Corn production in the eastern lowlands is hampered by a lack of machinery and traction animals. As a result, so much labor is required to produce corn that growers are unable to feed their families. Also, the low quality of land, from which tropical forest has been cleared, reduces yields and increases the labor required to produce corn. With increased population pressure, those using slash-and-burn planting techniques reduced the fallow period between plantings from as much as 20 years to two years. Thus, between 1982 and 1987, the area planted in corn increased by 20.6 percent, while output declined by 19.6 percent.[81]

The ban on timber cutting in eastern Chiapas, decreed for environmental reasons, also imposed a hardship on many small farmers who relied on occasional lumbering as a ready source of cash. As a result of this ban, peasants are frequently jailed for cutting one log, although large-scale, illegal logging continues.[82] Opportunities for growing crops for sale on the Mexican market were reduced by massive imports of food.[83] Opportunities for industrial employment were virtually non-existent. Chiapas ranks 23rd in industrialization among Mexican states, and average employment per employer is only 4.5.[84]

Since 1970, the per capita gross product has been declining in Chiapas. As government investment decreased in the 1980s, this decline accelerated. In the decade before the rebellion, per capita gross product in Chiapas declined at an annual rate of 6.5 percent, the highest such figure for any Mexican state.[85]

President Salinas' decision to amend Article 27 of the Mexican Constitution, and thus end land distribution and permit sale of *ejido* land, has already had a major psychological effect. Despite the flaws in the design and execution of land reform, its provisions did hold out hope to the landless that one day they might become landowners. Bishop Ruiz commented that the changes in Article 27 would result in a "breakdown of the sense of communal land ownership, concentration of ownership, and rural-to-urban migration."[86] Subcommander Marcos has declared that the constitutional changes were a major cause for the rebellion, since they caused people to give up hope of getting land by legal means.[87]

The changes in Article 27 not only dashed the aspirations of the landless but threatened those who already held ejido land. This is especially important in Chiapas, since 57 percent of the exploitable plots are either communal or form part of an ejido, the highest such figure for any Mexican state.[88] Holders of ejido land risk losing their land on the now-legalized market where they are at a conspicuous disadvantage compared to wealthy cattlemen. In addition, as they are aware, "land has been stolen from them by rapacious incomers, often under the complaisant eye of corrupt state officials and judges."[89]

In the late nineteenth century, much communally held Indian land in Chiapas was subdivided. Titles to the plots were distributed to Indians. Within a short period, such lands fell into the hands of large estate owners, leaving the Indians landless.[90]

The changes in Article 27 reflect the government's current market-oriented policies. As *El Financiero* editor Raymundo Riva Palacio comments:

> The naked capitalism unleashed by Salinas has not only affected Chiapas but the whole country. The administration's economic policies have resulted in the rich getting richer, while the lower-middle class, the working class, and the poor have become increasingly impoverished. Now the government must pay the piper.[91]

An easily quantifiable result of this "naked capitalism" is the number of billionaires (as measured in U.S. dollars) in Mexico. According to *Forbes* magazine, in 1990, there was only one. By 1994, there were 24.[92]

The final factor which led to the rebellion was the passage of the North American Free Trade Agreement (NAFTA). Farmers fear they will be overwhelmed by food imports from the United States, depriving them of their source of livelihood. This is especially true of corn producers. Corn producers feel threatened, since, given disadvantageous conditions, the production of a ton of corn in eastern Chiapas can take up to 300 days of labor. The Mexican average is eight days, and the U.S. average is 0.15 days.[93] Corn has immense symbolic as well as economic value. As Eduardo Pesqueira, Mexico's representative to the Food and Agricultural Organization (FAO), commented: "In Mexico, corn is more than a food. It is culture, religion, and national identity."[94]

The combination of skewed land ownership, unfavorable market ties, surplus labor, and government policy has led Chiapas to have some of the worst social indices in Mexico.

Chart 1: Social Indicators in Chiapas

	Percent of population	Ranking among the 31 Mexican states*
Illiterates older than 15	30.12	1
Population older than 15 who have not finished primary school	62.08	1
Population lacking toilets and sewage	42.66	5
Population lacking electricity	34.92	1
Population lacking running water	42.09	4
Population living in overcrowded housing	74.07	1
Population living in houses with dirt floors	50.90	2
Population living in communities of less than 5,000	66.56	3
Population making less than twice minimum wage	80.08	1

* 1 = worst Source: Vázquez Aguirre (1994: 27)

These lamentable statewide averages mask disparities within the state. A publication of the government anti-poverty program known as Solidarity notes:

> The population is kept in the same situation as in colonial times. Wealth, services, and power are concentrated in cities. *Criollos* and mestizos inhabit them. The rest of the population is concentrated in small dispersed communities where Indian peasants live.[95]

Illiteracy statistics indicate disparities within the state. In relatively privileged San Cristóbal, 25 percent of the residents are illiterate. In largely Indian Chamula, this figure reaches 71 percent.[96]

These indices often reflect deficiencies in government-supplied services. Many schools in areas inhabited by Indians only offer grades one to three.[97] The government has also slighted Chiapas in providing hospital services. The state has 0.3 hospital beds per 1,000 population, although the national average is 1.3.[98] Similarly, in Chiapas, there are 503 slots for recent medical-school graduates to perform required rural service. Such social service provides millions of rural Mexicans with their only access to health care. At the time of the rebellion, only 53 of these slots were filled, only two of which were in the Indian highlands.[99]

Despite spending more in Chiapas than in any other state, Solidarity failed to resolve the state's social problems. Solidarity's budget in Chiapas increased from $25 million in 1989 to $137 million in 1993. Its spending in Chiapas was characterized by: 1) corruption, 2) the rivalry between the traditional political elite and the new Solidarity bureaucracy, and 3) the overt political use of the program. Gov. González Garrido, for example, removed two Solidarity directors who allocated money to peasant groups independent of the PRI-controlled National Peasant Confederation. Some Solidarity spending reflects poor investment decisions. Examples include the little-used convention center in Tuxtla Gutiérrez and an expensive hospital sitting unused in Guadalupe Tepeyac.[100]

While many Solidarity projects are worthwhile, they fail to address the pressing need to give people an income. In desperately poor Chenalhó, Solidarity built a meeting hall and a public bath house. As commentator Héctor Díaz-Polanco noted, "I would claim that the rebellion did not break out despite Solidarity, but in part due to the effects of this program."[101]

Social change in Chiapas reflects social change at the national level. Despite Solidarity, the number of rural poor nationwide increased from 8.4 million in 1989 to 8.8 million in 1992. In 1992, Solidarity allocated 15 cents per poor Mexican per day. In Chiapas, only 13 cents was so allocated.[102]

Social conditions in Chiapas also reflect Mexican government investment priorities. The Federal District and the state of Nuevo León, which together have 13.95 percent of Mexico's population, receive 34.63 percent of government investment. The three poorest states, Guerrero, Oaxaca, and Chiapas, which together have 10.89 percent of Mexico's population, only receive 8.32 percent of government investment.[103]

Chapter 2: The Uprising

The world greeted the 1994 New Year with images of masked rebels occupying San Cristóbal de las Casas, the political, economic, and religious center for the largely indigenous highlands. Rebels also occupied the municipal seats in Ocosingo, Las Margaritas, and Altamirano, the local power centers for eastern Chiapas. In Ocosingo and San Cristóbal, land records, frequently used to buttress cattlemen's land claims, were destroyed. The rebels released 230 prisoners from four different jails. Jailers, fearing retribution, put on prison garb and departed unharmed along with their former charges. Many of those released were indigenous people jailed as a result of land disputes.[104]

An observer in San Cristóbal described the rebels who occupied the city on 1 January:

> They're mostly dark-skinned and many of them are young women. Some of them are younger than 16 years. They tally about 150 of them. They all have on a red bandanna around their neck and they had risen the flag above the palace there, but they're just sort of very solemn and determined looking, and they have their sort of stashes of powdered milk there and—eating their tortillas, and they seem to be very poor and mostly young.[105]

Given the element of surprise, the rebels met little resistance on the first. In most places, including San Cristóbal, rebels simply entered the center of town and took over.

At 1:00 a.m. on New Year's Day, Amado Avendaño, editor of the San Cristóbal paper *Tiempo*, received a telephone call inquiring if there were problems in the city. As a good newspaperman, he called

VILLAGES OF HIGHLAND CHIAPAS

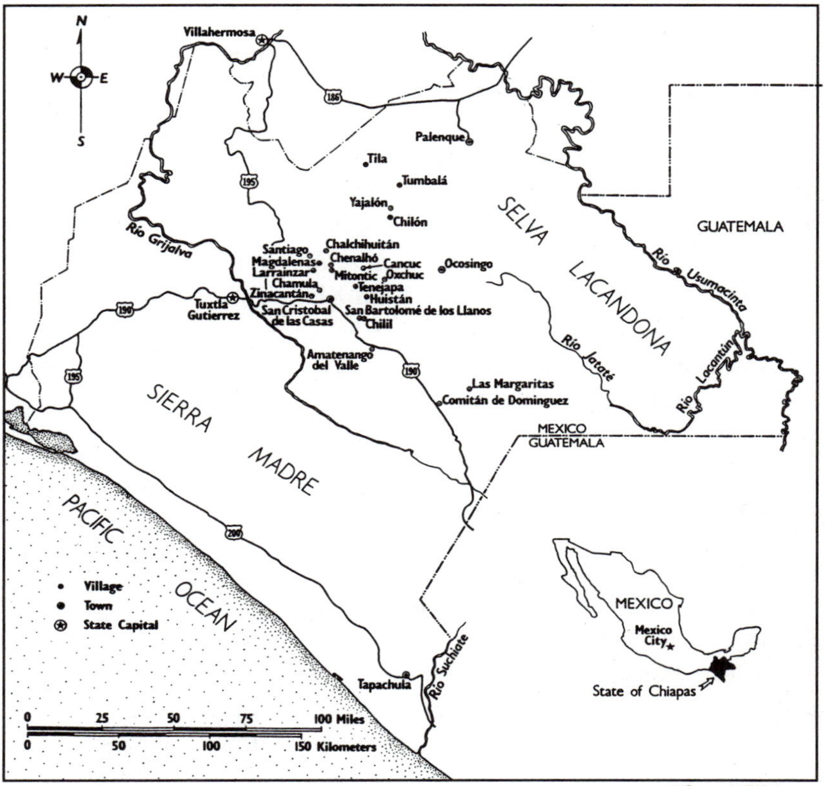

JVCotter & JDNations

the nearby military base at Ranch Nuevo to follow up on the inquiry. He was told that everything was fine. The military, however, wondered why they had received such an inquiry. To be on the safe side, they called the police station in San Cristóbal to inquire if there were any problems. Subcommander Marcos answered the phone there and assured the worried caller that everything was fine. The military remained in its barracks that night.[106]

On the second, the rebels withdrew from San Cristóbal rather than face the vastly superior firepower of the Mexican army. They left behind painted slogans such as, "Death to the bourgeoisie! Long live the poor!" Another slogan referred to the military base at Rancho Nuevo: "We've gone on to Rancho Nuevo, then to Tuxtla. From now on, there will be no rest."[107] That day, 16 rebels were killed when a helicopter fired on a small bus they had commandeered.[108] That afternoon, troops began to arrive in Chiapas by helicopter. According the Defense Ministry, 29 people died on 2 January, including five members of the Mexican army.[109]

The most intense New Year's Day combat occurred in Ocosingo. For eight hours, roughly 400 Zapatistas battled 20 to 30 state judicial police to take the city hall. Once the city hall was taken, Zapatistas broke open the ISSSTE store, which serves government employees, and La Suriana, another large store, and distributed merchandise to residents. Rebels occupied radio station XEOCH there and broadcast *ranchero* music and political messages.

A second battle occurred when government forces recaptured the Ocosingo market, where rebels had gathered. The Defense Ministry reported that seven soldiers, 27 civilians, and 59 rebels were killed in Ocosingo.[110]

The rebels had planned to evacuate Ocosingo, just as they had evacuated San Cristóbal. They boarded the same trucks which had brought them to town and headed down the road toward Palenque. Since they expected government troops to advance from San Cristóbal, the rebels left snipers to delay them. However, when they encountered an unexpected army column approaching from Palenque, the rebels retreated and attempted to defend the market in Ocosingo. This decision—to hold the market rather than to simply abandon their vehicles and scatter—was the rebels' most serious military blunder. It left them in a fixed position exposed to superior government firepower, including machine-gun-equipped helicopters.[111]

After the government had retaken the city, a reporter commented: "The stench of death permeates Ocosingo. The buzzards smell it and circle, looking for dead meat, while helicopters circle, looking for live meat."[112]

Three thousand government troops moved into San Cristóbal on the third. That night, Secretary of Defense Antonio Riviello reported that the four municipal seats which had been occupied by the rebels were back under government control.

Through the end of the first week of January, there were continued reports of combat in several locations. In addition, government helicopters and planes attacked populated areas south of San Cristóbal with machine guns and explosives.[113]

In Oxchuc, events took a unique turn. Eleven rebels there were captured and beaten by local residents as they attempted to flee from the army. The rebels were then turned over to authorities. This was done by those who have a stake in the status quo. Many such individuals had well-paying jobs outside their home villages in the 1970s and early 1980s. They then returned with their earnings and invested in fertilizer, pesticides, and other green-revolution techniques. This stratified communities economically and left some opposed to change. It left others further behind.[114]

By the second week of January, combat had largely ceased. In part this resulted from inclement weather which hampered military operations.[115] In addition, rather than facing the estimated 17,000 troops who had arrived in the state, most rebels moved back into the forest. The most significant combat of the second week was at Rancho Nuevo, 10 kilometers southeast of San Cristóbal de las Casas. Rancho Nuevo, which serves as command post of the 31st Military District, was attacked for eight consecutive days. Subcommander Marcos later noted that these attacks pinned the army down, thus permitting rebels in other areas to retreat without interference from the military.[116]

Casualty estimates vary. The National Commission for Human Rights (CNDH) placed the number of dead at 159. They included 16 members of the Mexican army, 38 police, 67 civilians, and 38 unidentified individuals.[117] The International Committee of Jurists estimated the number of dead at between 200 and 300.[118] The rebels reported that, up until 2 February, their casualties were more than 500 dead, 300 disappeared, 370 taken prisoner, and 50 wounded.[119]

The smoke of battle had hardly cleared before accusations of human-rights violations began to pour in. There is a widely shared view that the military used excessive force, including aerial attacks on inhabited areas without a clear military objective and firing on press vehicles when no rebels were in sight.[120] The prominent role played by Mexican human-rights observers highlighted a recent trend in Mexico—the increasingly important role of non-governmental organizations.

One widely reported incident involved the Ejido Morelia, in the municipality of Altamirano. A resident there commented: "We are more afraid of the army than of the Zapatistas, because they treat us like animals." The army looted the town's store, robbed homes, and forced the ejido's 150 men to lie down on the basketball court. Soldiers then walked on the residents and tortured them. Three men were carried off by the military. Their bodies were later found in a nearby gully.[121]

A report issued by Amnesty International noted that members of the Mexican army and security forces were responsible for at least nine extrajudicial killings, 15 other suspicious killings, and scores of arbitrary detentions. One of the members of the Amnesty team, Morris Tidball, commented that the events in Chiapas were "yet another chapter in the pattern of chronic violence and impunity which exists in rural Mexico, particularly in areas where there are Indians with little or no access to land."[122]

A report issued by Human Rights Watch/Americas noted that army sweeps of many towns and hamlets led to deaths and injuries to civilians as well as massive arrests. Those detained were subject to torture, cruel treatment, and prolonged detention in violation of Mexican law. Human Rights Watch/Americas also found the rebel force had violated laws of war by using civilians as shields during combat, destroying non-military targets, taking hostages, and, in one case, murdering a hostage.[123]

The government National Commission for Human Rights (CNDH) noted that it had received 76 complaints against the army and four against agents of the federal attorney general's office, as well as nine against state and municipal officials.[124] Human-rights activist Allan Nairn also noted that both sides engaged in human-rights abuses. He cited numerous government abuses, as well as rebel abuses such as forced recruitment and kidnappings, including that of former Gov. Absalón Castellanos Domínguez.[125]

The CNDH not only reported on human-rights abuses in Chiapas but became the subject of sharp criticism for its role there. For example, Concepción Villafuerte Blanco, editor of the San Cristóbal newspaper *Tiempo*, commented: "The role of the CNDH in my opinion is shameful. They have violated human rights along with the army. If CNDH members ride in army helicopters, how are they going to complain about the military? They are protected by police and soldiers."[126]

Chapter 3: Responses to the Uprising

Official responses to the uprising attempted to shift blame away from those who had designed flawed government policy. There was also an unwillingness to acknowledge that conditions were so bad that the indigenous population of Chiapas had rebelled. Rather, blame was placed on others for misleading or beguiling the Indians.

Initial responses to the uprising were surprisingly conciliatory. On 1 January, Ricardo García Villalobos, subsecretary of the interior, declared: "The Mexican government calls on these groups to be prudent, to change their attitude, and to began a dialogue within legal channels. Government officials have been willing and are still willing to begin such a dialogue." He also observed, "This region has historically suffered from backwardness which still has not been totally eliminated, despite the great efforts made during the five years of this administration."[127]

Also on the first, Chiapas Gov. Elmar Setzer attempted to place blame for the uprising: "Direct reports from residents of these municipalities indicate that some of the Catholic priests espousing liberation theology and their deacons linked themselves to these groups and provided support through the use of the radio network of the Diocese of San Cristóbal."[128]

A bulletin from the Interior Ministry, issued on 2 January, was still conciliatory. The term "armed group" was used four times to describe the rebel force (EZLN), and "aggressor" was used three times. The bulletin did not refer to the EZLN by name.[129] The government soon settled on the term "transgressors" to describe the rebels.

On the third, President Salinas responded to the crisis, noting, "We will always seek the rule of law, peaceful dialogue, and, in particular, defense of human rights in all aspects of community life."

El Financiero editor Riva Palacio commented that President Salinas was seemingly losing touch, since what he described was the exact opposite of the conditions which had prevailed in Chiapas.[130]

By 3 January, the Interior Ministry was much less conciliatory and stated that the events in Chiapas resulted from Mexican and foreign interests tied to violent groups in Central America.[131]

On the fifth, a joint declaration of the Interior, Defense, and Social Development ministries, as well as the attorney general's office, noted that what occurred in Chiapas was not an Indian uprising but one led by Mexican and foreign professionals.[132] Also on the fifth, Eloy Cantú Segovia, an official of the Interior Ministry, offered the rebels a cease-fire if they would: 1) cease hostilities, 2) lay down their arms and return 1,500 kilograms of dynamite stolen from the government oil company Pemex on 31 December, 3) release all captives and hostages, and 4) identify their leaders.[133]

On 5 January, President Salinas declared the rebellion was caused by "those who make a profession of violence, Mexicans and a group of foreigners." He also stated: "This is not an Indian uprising, but the action of a violent, armed group, directed against public peace and government institutions."[134]

On the seventh, the Interior Ministry released a 28-page report on the EZLN, reporting that the government was still willing to negotiate and offering amnesty to those who had been forced into joining. The report also declared that the EZLN was led by Mexicans and foreigners who have "manipulated disaffected persons and those who live under adverse conditions."[135]

The government became less conciliatory early in the second week of January. On the eighth, the attorney general's office declared that the presumed leaders of the rebellion included priests, a sergeant of the Salvadoran army, and members of the center-left Party of the Democratic Revolution (PRD).[136] The next day, the Interior Ministry published a two-page statement in the paper *Excélsior*. It claimed that Mexican and foreign leaders of the movement were "violent and aggressive" and that local participants were manipulated or pressured into taking part. The statement declared that the rebellion "is not an indigenous movement nor is it a peasant action."[137]

Some members of the government took an even harder line. For example, on 10 January, long-time labor leader Fidel Velázquez urged that the rebels be "exterminated." He declared that the rebels had "no justifiable complaints against the government" and blamed the uprising on Peruvians, Salvadorans, Guatemalans, and Nicaraguans.[138] Velázquez later charged that the PRD was behind the uprising and said the media was siding with the rebel cause by criticizing army excesses.[139]

Later in the second week of January, the government position once again became more conciliatory. One of the factors producing this was the dynamiting of electrical transmission lines in Puebla and Michoacán on 6 January. In addition, a bomb exploded in Plaza Universidad, a Mexico City shopping center.[140] On the eighth, a car-bomb blew up 500 meters from Campo Militar Número Uno in the Federal District. These attacks, presumably by sympathizers of the rebels in Chiapas, raised the specter of the Chiapas revolt spreading into other areas of the country.

A second factor leading to conciliation was the level of scrutiny which government actions received nationally and internationally. Television viewers worldwide saw pictures of aerial attacks on inhabited hillsides and poor rural residents.[141] At the same time, activists throughout North America were exchanging information by fax and e-mail, using contacts developed during their campaign against the North American Free Trade Agreement. This information was shared with the public, often at demonstrations in front of Mexican consulates.[142]

A third factor leading to a more conciliatory approach toward the EZLN was the government's own standing in public opinion. As historian Lorenzo Meyer noted: "To carry out a prolonged war against the EZLN supported by most Mexicans, the government needs consensus, and above all, legitimacy, both of which have been lacking for some time."[143]

Finally, the government was under pressure to make a conciliatory response since, in a communiqué issued on 6 January, the rebels expressed a willingness to negotiate with the government if: 1) the government would recognize the EZLN as a belligerent force, 2) both sides would agree to a cease-fire, 3) federal troops would be withdrawn from rebel areas and returned to their home barracks, and 4) the military would cease bombing rural areas.[144]

Conciliation was the cornerstone of Salinas' strategy. Author César Romero Jacobo concluded that Salinas' goals were to: 1) keep the conflict regional, 2) open up the political system enough to keep intact his reputation as a conciliator, and 3) keep the Mexican army loyal and cohesive.[145]

On 10 January, Salinas appointed as his chief negotiator Manuel Camacho Solís, the former mayor of Mexico City. He was given the title of Commissioner for Peace and Reconciliation. At the time of his appointment, Salinas commented on Camacho Solís' role: "He will have the support of and permanent access to the president. He will seek to open dialogue which will contribute to generalized reconciliation in Chiapas."[146]

Two days after appointing Camacho Solís, Salinas declared a cease-fire and offered rebels an amnesty. Salinas declared, "I fervently desire that this decision of the government, which reflects the sentiments of Mexican society, will result in saving lives and finding new ways to reconciliation."[147] The Defense Ministry reported that, in the three days following the cease-fire, there was only one incident which involved "a group of transgressors" who fired on soldiers carrying out reconnaissance near Ocosingo.[148]

The rebels responded to the cease-fire with the following declaration:

> Today, 12 January 1994, we learned that Carlos Salinas de Gortari, in his role as commander-in-chief of the army, ordered a cease-fire. ... The Clandestine Indigenous Revolutionary Committee, which commands the Zapatista National Liberation Army, welcomes this decision and sees it as a first step to dialogue between the belligerents. ... However, what Salinas decreed is only a first step. ... We will not lay down our arms and surrender our forces to the bad government.[149]

Negotiator Camacho Solís also reflected the government's conciliatory stance. At a press conference in San Cristóbal on 13 January, he declared: "If we want to lay the foundation for peace, we have to take into account the complexity and uniqueness of what is happening here. If we don't, we're not going to make any progress."[150]

Even after Camacho Solís had been designated as negotiator, the government continued to place the blame on outsiders. On 15 January, the Social Development Ministry commented that poverty was only a "pretext" and that the uprising was "a political-military movement implanted among the Indians, but not representing them."[151]

Despite the government's unwillingness to accept failed policy as a cause of the rebellion, as philosopher Leopoldo Zea commented, the government's declaration of a unilateral cease-fire and its willingness to negotiate were a far less brutal way to resolve the crisis than the prolonged combat that had plagued Central America in the 1970s and 1980s.[152]

Bishop Ruiz, who was chosen to mediate the negotiations, commented on the negotiating process in his homily of 23 January:

> Peace in our country, which we thought was so solid, showed its fragility. This fragility resulted from its being based on injustice, which we still have not overcome. We suffered through moments of anguish in the first days of the year. The events jolted our conscience. The fear that an uncontrollable spiral of violence might have been touched off has given way to the urgent need for establishing a forum for negotiating a peace with justice. With great hope, we are preparing the ground for such a peace. ... In searching for peace, we must be guided by a generous, magnanimous love, ready for forgiveness and reconciliation. Brotherly love and the love for life are

Bishop Samuel Ruiz *Paulina Hermosillo*

> the highest values of our Christian faith and are present in Christ's example. They should overcome feelings of rancor and vengeance. We are now in the historical moment in which this love can manifest itself in all its glory. Thus, this time of crisis will become a time of grace.[153]

Salinas' pardon offer of 12 January was specifically directed at "those who have participated in the rebellion due to pressure or deception and who now accept peace and legality." In a response that was widely quoted in Mexico, Marcos replied to the pardon offer:

> For what do we have to ask forgiveness? For what are we to be pardoned? For not dying of hunger? For not suffering in silent misery? For not humbly accepting our historical burden of scorn and abandonment? For having taken up arms when all other paths were closed off? For not respecting the penal code of Chiapas, the most absurd and repressive in memory? For having shown the rest of the country and the entire world that Chiapas' poverty-stricken residents still have human dignity? For having prepared ourselves thoroughly before January first? For having used rifles to fight with instead of bows and arrows? For having trained before going into combat? For all of us being Mexican? For most of us being Indians? For having called on the Mexican people to struggle by whatever means were at their disposal for what is rightfully theirs? For having fought for liberty, democracy, and justice? For not following the example of previous guerrilla groups? For not surrendering? For not selling out? For not betraying ourselves? Who must ask for pardon and who can grant it?[154]

This in turn moved conservative, Nobel prize-winning author Octavio Paz to write:

> The eloquent letter that Subcommander Marcos sent to various newspapers on 18 January truly moved me, even though it was sent by someone who has taken a course of action of which I disapprove. They, the Indians of Mexico, are not the ones who should ask for pardon. Rather, we are the ones who should ask for pardon. I don't close my eyes to the responsibility of our authorities, especially those in Chiapas. Nor do I

> close my eyes to the equally serious problem—the egotism and narrow-mindedness of the wealthy in that rich province. This responsibility also extends to all of Mexican society. Almost all of us, to one degree or another, are guilty of the iniquitous situation in which the Indians find themselves, since our passivity and indifference have permitted the extortions and abuses of the cattlemen, coffee growers, caciques, and corrupt politicians.[155]

In addition to government comments on the uprising, there were comments from virtually every other sector of society. The presidential candidates were inevitably forced to respond to the situation in Chiapas. On 2 January, Luis Colosio, candidate of the incumbent Party of the Institutionalized Revolution (PRI), stated that unmet social needs "are not a valid reason to opt for violence, disturb the social order, and erode the social peace. ..."[156] The following week, Colosio worked the theme of reform into the inauguration of his presidential campaign. He stated: "The events in Chiapas are a call to the conscience of all Mexicans. They indicate the urgent need for social justice. They also show us how absurd violence is."[157]

National Action Party (PAN) presidential candidate Diego Fernández de Cevallos also commented on the rebellion: "The causes are injustice and marginalization. But this does not justify groups surreptitiously acquiring sophisticated arms to put into the hands of peasants. This is a crime which should not go unpunished."[158] He also stated that the government should not negotiate with the criminal groups that organized the peasant rebels, but only with "true peasants."[159]

On the first, Cuauhtémoc Cárdenas, the PRD's presidential candidate, commented, "Violence, regardless of where it comes from, only leads to the shedding of blood, destruction, and even more social problems." He added that the correct way to produce change was through elections, despite their past shortcomings.[160] Cárdenas was the only major candidate to use the uprising to attack the incumbents. He noted that the uprising was "the product of infrahuman conditions of oppression, misery, hunger, privation, and denial of democratic and human rights. Such conditions have been imposed on the state and in particular on its indigenous people by the regime of the PRI and of Carlos Salinas de Gortari."[161]

Chapter 4: The Roots of the Movement

> This peasant war, the current incarnation of a tradition of cyclic Indian revolts, grew out of nearly 20 years of political agitation in the countryside, primarily over land.
>
> — Luis Hernández Navarro[162]

The rebel force which burst into the world's consciousness on New Year's Day 1994 emerged from a rich assortment of autonomous peasant organizations which sprang up during the 1970s and 1980s. These movements in turn were shaped by churches (especially the Catholic Church), the government (especially the National Indigenous Institute, or INI), trade unions (especially the teachers' union), and Mexican political organizers from outside Chiapas.[163]

One of the early influences was pastoral activity organized by the Catholic diocese of San Cristóbal in the 1960s and 1970s. Lay teachers known as catechists fanned out to some 200 localities. They were influenced by liberation theology, which at the time was an important current in Latin American Catholicism. The catechists organized base communities and encouraged people in Chiapas to openly articulate economic and social demands with the aim of improving their lot in society.[164]

As with subsequent organizers, many catechists remained for decades. A Tzotzil interviewed during the first week of the uprising commented: "When I was a child, the catechists taught me the Our Father and the Hail Mary. ... The same catechists from more than 20 years ago invited us to join the Zapatista army early on the morning of January first."[165]

The Catholic Church also helped organize the First Indigenous Congress held in San Cristóbal in October 1974. It was attended by members of various Indian groups representing 327 communities, including 587 Tzeltals, 330 Tzotzils, 152 Tojolabals, and 161 Chols. The most frequently heard demand at the congress was, "Give us back the land which they have taken." Those attending also demanded they be given title to ejido land and denounced the failure to enforce the minimum-wage provisions of the Federal Labor Code. They also demanded better market access. This reflected the control of marketing by intermediaries who allocate credit, provide transportation, and set prices. Other demands included education in Indian languages and preservation of Indian culture. Finally, congress attendees sought better medical services. Although there was little concrete response to the demands, the congress did lay the groundwork for the grass-roots organizing that continues to this day.[166]

It is not surprising that land matters dominated the congress. The previous year, a survey had found that only 36 families in Ocosingo, many with estates dating back to colonial times or to the administration of Porfirio Díaz (1876-1911), owned more than 300,000 hectares of land.[167] Such landowners were, however, not content with their massive holdings. While the dispossessed were demanding the subdivision of large estates, ranchers were still invading ejidos and government land and appropriating it for their own.[168]

Beginning in the late 1960s, Maoist political organizers began arriving in Chiapas. Two of the groups represented were the People's Union (*Unión del Pueblo*) and Popular Politics (*Política Popular*). Following the Maoist notion of "insertion among the masses," the organizers maintained a low profile, worked directly with peasants, and remained for years.[169] This diaspora into the Mexican hinterlands was typical of the Mexican left after the massacre of students in Mexico City in 1968. The arrival of organizers with a political agenda continued into the 1980s.[170]

Marcos stated that he had arrived in Chiapas as an organizer in 1983. He commented on his experience:

> We felt invincible. We felt with our pure conviction we could defeat any army. We began to speak with the communities, from which we received an important lesson. The democratic organization and social life of the indigenous people is very honorable, very transparent. It is very hard to ignore reality and become corrupt. We saw many people die, including

> many children. They died in our arms while we were carrying out the health campaign that the government didn't undertake and which we had to.[171]

Teachers also exercised a strong political influence on Chiapas. They initially addressed demands such as trade-union democracy and higher wages. However, in Chiapas, the teachers' movement made a specific commitment to organize rural residents about issues not directly related to education. Such teachers served as grass-roots intellectuals for the emerging peasant organizations. Much of the teachers' effort was aimed at obtaining a higher guaranteed price for corn. The movement was suppressed and its leaders were jailed, since they were viewed as a threat to the status quo.[172]

By the late 1970s, peasants were organizing their own groups without outside input. The Catholic Church lost influence, in part due to the movements' becoming more radical. Attacks by ranchers on organized peasants contributed to this radicalization.[173] As peasants grew more radical, their tactics changed. As early as 1974, a thousand Indians attacked estates in the municipality of El Bosque, killing seven landowners. The army intervened to remove the Indians.[174] Others occupied municipal buildings, seized cattle, and blocked roads.[175]

A few joined armed guerrilla groups in the 1970s. These groups were strongly influenced by their ties to political groups outside Chiapas. They later dissolved without directly confronting the army.[176] The best known of these small groups was the Armed Forces of National Liberation (FALN), which operated near Ocosingo. It was led by César Yáñez, otherwise known as Brother Pedro.[177]

The 1980s saw a proliferation of peasant organizations. Their profusion reflects the diversity of the state and different strategies for producing change. Anthropologist Neil Harvey notes that the state is made up of nine distinct zones, each with its own geography, crops, and ethnic makeup.[178] The organizations also reflected the social differences among the rural poor of Chiapas. Some produced crops on their own land and marketed them. Such individuals had specific demands, depending on the crop they grew, concerning price, marketing, and credit. Others sharecropped. Still others worked for wages. Petty commerce and handicrafts provided additional employment. Many individuals and families engaged in a combination of these activities.

The organizations were of three general types. Some were regional, such as the Independent Farmworkers and Peasants Central (CIOAC). They encompassed several municipalities and operated in areas where wage labor dominated. Others functioned at the municipal level, generally in more traditional areas. They usually focused on struggles against a cacique. Still others, most frequently in the east, involved a community pitted against a single cattleman or lumberman. These were the struggles which most often turned violent.[179]

One of the groups of the early 1980s was the Rural Association of Collective Interest (ARIC). Members of this group advocated change through the institutional route. They sought to negotiate with the government and ensure that laws on the books were actually enforced. Given the limited success achieved by those taking the institutional route, peasants increasingly turned to more militant groups.[180]

Another significant group of the 1980s was the Union of Ejido Unions and Solidarity Groups of Chiapas. This was an umbrella group of 12,000 families, most of whom were indigenous, from 180 communities in 11 municipalities.[181] A second major group was the CIOAC, which concentrated on organizing day laborers. This regional group formed unions in the northern part of the state. Another major group was initially called the Communalists of the Municipality of Venustiano Carranza. Later it took the name Emiliano Zapata Peasant Organization (OCEZ). It concentrated on obtaining land and combating repression.[182] From November 1986 to 1990, there were 72 reported land occupations. Peasants were later expelled from 69 of the occupied areas.[183]

The results of decades of peasant organizing became apparent on 12 October 1992, the 500th anniversary of the arrival of Christopher Columbus in the New World. Ten thousand Indians marched in San Cristóbal, not to celebrate Columbus' arrival, but to honor 500 years of Indian resistance. The marchers toppled the statue of Diego de Mazariegos, the Spanish conqueror of Chiapas. Roughly half of those marching were members of the Emiliano Zapata National Independent Peasant Alliance (ANCIEZ), a peasant group founded in 1989.[184]

By the end of 1990, it had become clear that, despite massive organization and well-articulated demands, peasant organizations were making little headway. Their members were often attacked by gunmen hired by local cattlemen. In addition, politicians and cattlemen cooperated to minimize the cost of land and labor for major landowners.[185] While peasant organizations met with limited success in achieving their demands, they were crucial in opening the way for the EZLN. As anthropologist Andrés Fábregas noted:

> The ties the rebels have to the political organizations which have sprung up in the jungle in recent years are fundamental for their analysis. It should be noted that it is not poverty alone which touched off the uprising. If that were true, the highlands would have been the area of the uprising, since it is the most marginalized area of the state.[186]

Starting in 1991, groups of people disappeared for days at a time for unexplained reasons. They would then return home and plunge back into social organizations, stressing the need for a "real" organization. By 1993, a perceptive observer would have noted a series of behavioral changes. Residents of the areas which were to rebel reduced their contacts with the government. Coffee plantations were abandoned. Unusually large amounts of cattle were sold. Increasingly, loans by the government agency Solidarity were not being repaid. Children quit going to school. Indians began to lose their fear of landowners. They no longer stood silently looking at their feet when in the landowners' presence. Such behavior spread into the highlands, especially among those engaged in long, and generally fruitless, struggles against caciques.[187]

Early in 1993, the ANCIEZ went underground.[188] Evidence of armed organization came to light in March 1993, when two soldiers were killed at San Isidro El Ocotal. That month a government official in Las Margaritas wrote a letter reporting there were guerrillas in the area. Two more soldiers were killed between Ocosingo and Altamirano in May 1993.[189] Upon investigating, the military found training camps with mock streets laid out, complete with wooden vehicles so that rural people could train for urban combat.[190] Despite the letter, government casualties, and the discovery of the training camp, Interior Secretary (and former Chiapas governor)

González Garrido responded to concern about guerrillas in Chiapas:

> To spread this false rumor will cause serious damage to the development of the state, since it will block domestic and foreign investment in the agricultural sector. The government of Mexico rejects the possibility of a guerrilla force in this southern Mexican state, or of any other group which is planning an uprising due to the marginalization of the peasants and Indians.[191]

Several explanations have been offered to explain why the government did not make a pre-emptive strike against the rebel force before 1994. They include: 1) a failure to realize how large the EZLN force was, 2) the failure of local officials to convey information concerning the movement to the national level, and 3) fear that any attack would have destroyed the image Mexico was trying to present to the world and thus prevent the passage of NAFTA in the U.S. Congress. Subcommander Marcos feels the failure to act resulted from fear of upsetting NAFTA negotiations.[192]

An earlier uprising would have likely prevented passage of NAFTA, but would have left the government free to carry out a scorched-earth policy in Chiapas, similar to what happened just across the border in Guatemala. However, once NAFTA was passed, the situation changed. As journalist Marc Cooper noted: "With Big Trading Brother's eyes cast southward, the Mexican army would have to restrain itself."[193] Another interpretation is that the uprising was originally timed for November 1993, but had to be postponed to provide an opportunity to relocate training camps after they were discovered earlier in the year.[194]

Chapter 5: The Zapatista National Liberation Army

> Armed popular uprisings of peasants don't just appear overnight. Their long incubation period makes them resistant to sudden repression. These armed peasant uprisings don't always have enough impact to destabilize society as a whole, but they do show great resistance, which, over the course of centuries, has been one of their distinctive characteristics.
>
> — Carlos Montemayor, 1994[195]

When their January 1994 offensive began, the rebels published a declaration of war. It concluded:

> To the Mexican People:
>
> We, honest, free men and women, believe that the war we are declaring is our last hope and that it is just and necessary. For many years, dictators have been engaged in an undeclared genocidal war against our people. For this reason, we ask for your participation and support in our struggle for *jobs, land, housing, food, health, education, independence, liberty, democracy, and justice and peace.* We will not stop fighting until these basic demands are met and a free and democratic government rules in Mexico.[196]

This declaration was widely circulated both nationally and internationally. It was only the first example of the rebels' effective use of the media. The rebels not only held a press conference in San Cristóbal on 1 January, but immediately began faxing press releases in English and Spanish.[197]

The Zapatistas' message was not only disseminated effectively, but it was easily understandable. Historian Meyer feels this is one of the reasons for the EZLN's widespread support. He comments: "The political discourse of the new Zapatistas is simple, comprehensible, and has a clear moral basis. Thus, it is the antithesis of the language used by the government."[198]

The armed movement adopted the name Zapatista National Liberation Army (EZLN). Emiliano Zapata had been a peasant leader in the Mexican Revolution of 1910. When asked why his name had been chosen for the movement, "Mario," the rebel leader in the taking of Ocosingo, responded: "Because he was a peasant leader. He was the one who wanted to give us land. But he was later killed by the bourgeoisie."[199]

The declaration of war revealed the EZLN's nationalism. Rather than referring to class struggle, Cuba, or Central America, it stated that the rebellion was the product of the long tradition which began with Mexicans' struggle against slavery during the colonial period and which continued with the War of Independence, the Mexican Revolution, and the 1968 student movement. It also claimed to be legalistic. It labeled the Salinas de Gortari administration as a "dictatorship," and noted that, according to Article 39 of the Mexican Constitution, "the people have, at all times, the inalienable right to alter or modify their form of government."

On 6 January, the rebels issued a communiqué which distinguished the EZLN from other 20th-century Latin American insurgencies. Rather than declaring that the EZLN wanted to take state power to further its goals, it called for President Salinas de Gortari's "illegitimate government" to resign to permit the formation of "a transitional democratic government which will guarantee clean elections throughout the county at all levels of government." The communiqué also stated that only with a functioning democracy would it be possible to "improve the economic and social conditions of Mexico's dispossessed."[200]

Subcommander Marcos raised another demand in a February interview—Indian autonomy. He declared that regions with a large indigenous population should have their own governments. He stated: "What the government has to do is recognize that our form of government will be the one which makes decisions. It has to respect it and not interfere with it."[201] Another unidentified Indian leader commented: "We want our culture to be respected, our languages, our way of life, and, especially, our land. The land is our mother. She feeds us, she shelters us, she sustains us for our whole life, and they even want to take that away from us."[202]

Another demand, which Marcos attributed to the Clandestine Indian Revolutionary Committee (CCRI), was that changes in ejido legislation be reversed. Article 27, as amended in 1992, permits the sale of ejido land. Marcos noted: "The comrades say that land is life, that if you don't have land, you're living dead, and so why live. It's better to fight and die fighting."[203]

Some rebel demands address material needs. Others relate to the status of the Indians. An unidentified rebel commented, "We aren't asking the government to give us a piece of candy, or bread, or a T-shirt, as they have in the past, but for liberty, democracy, and justice."[204]

While the EZLN's demands have been widely circulated, there is much less certainty about other aspects of the EZLN, given its clandestine nature. Anthropologist Neil Harvey estimates the number

Zapatistas *Paulina Hermosillo*

of rebels at 3,000 to 4,000 and feels that most of them come from indigenous communities in the eastern region of Chiapas.[205] Other estimates place the size of the rebel forces as high as 8,000.[206] In an interview, when asked how many rebels he commanded, Mario simply declared, "*Somos un chingo* (There's lots of us)."[207]

Journalist Alma Guillermoprieto feels that the members of the EZLN are not the poorest people of Chiapas—those tied to exhausted hillside farms by tradition and passivity. Rather, EZLN members are "the innovators: adventurous frontiersmen and women who were convinced that they could make a new world."[208] Similarly, historian Antonio García de León notes that, rather than being made up of traditional peasant farmers, "the Zapatista army is made up principally of marginal 'modern' young people, who are multilingual and who have experience performing wage labor. They have very little in common with the isolated Indian that we here in Mexico City imagine."[209]

The role of women within the EZLN reflects changes occurring in Chiapan society. Many women have assumed leadership roles during the recent past—organizing co-ops and health-care facilities, confronting authorities, and moving with their families to the sparsely inhabited east. Anthropologist Rosalva Aída Hernández Castillo comments on the result: "Within these processes of transformation, many Indian women have, rather than rejecting the traditional, redefined it along new lines." Reflecting their newly found awareness, early in 1994, women organized the Congress of Indigenous and Peasant Women of Chiapas, which was attended by members of various artisan and peasant groups.[210]

These new roles are reflected within the EZLN. As Marcos noted: "The EZLN is composed of about two-thirds men and one-third women. It is very common to have military units where the only woman is the commander. The entire unit, all of her subordinates, are men. This caused many problems before 1 January."[211]

The documents released by the rebels on New Year's Day included a Revolutionary Women's Law. This 10-point decree stated that women have the right to assume any position within the struggle that their abilities merit. The law also decreed women's right to a "just" salary, their right to determine the number of children desired, to choose a spouse, to hold leadership positions in the EZLN, to not be physically abused, to participate in the community, to education, and to health care for themselves and their children.[212]

Marcos stated that women feel change is likely to come from their own actions, rather than from formal decrees. He stated, "That's why in our list of demands to the government, it doesn't mention anything about gender. The compañeras say: 'We aren't going to ask the government to give us freedom, nor are we going to ask you male fools. We are going to ensure our freedom, our respect, and our dignity as women, as human beings.'"[213]

Three Indians and three non-Indians founded the EZLN in 1982. Unlike many earlier Latin American guerrilla groups, the Chiapas rebels had no supply line running from urban areas to rebel camps. Supplies were so short in the early days that the rebels caught animals in traps to save on bullets. After four years, the group only numbered sixty.[214]

The EZLN, like other Latin American rebel groups, began as a vanguard organization; that is, its members simply declared rebel authority. However, local Indians, despite agreeing with the rebels' critique of Mexican society, were unwilling to put their fate in the hands of a group of ragtag newcomers. The rebels soon realized that wholehearted support by the local population would require giving that population the final say as to what the rebels would do.

The rebels thus accepted community control—making the Chiapas rebellion unique. Marcos said of this decision, "I feel we hit the nail on the head when we decided to surrender power, when we said, 'Clearly, it's better for us to let them decide what to do.' That is when the EZLN began to broaden its range and grow explosively."[215]

While acceptance of grass-roots control greatly facilitated recruiting, it dispersed power. Each zone and valley had its own army. To overcome this dispersal, the Clandestine Indian Revolutionary Committee (CCRI) was formed to serve as an overall command structure. It is composed exclusively of representatives of such indigenous groups as the Tzotzil, Tzeltal, Chol, and Tojolabal.

The ethnic makeup of the CCRI reflects the ethnic makeup of the EZLN. The rebels' 6 January communiqué stated: "The majority of the EZLN troops are indigenous people from the state of Chiapas. This is the case because we, the indigenous people, represent the most humiliated and dispossessed sector in Mexico, but also, as you can see, the most dignified." The same communiqué noted that other members of the EZLN were Chiapan non-Indians of the same social strata and some individuals from other Mexican states.

An obvious example of a non-Indian is Subcommander Marcos. When asked why Marcos was chosen as the public representative of the EZLN, an unidentified Indian declared: "*Marcos tiene la facilidad del castilla. Nosotros todavía fallan un chingo. Por eso necesitamos que haga muchas cositas para nosotros.* (Marcos has the ability to speak Spanish. We still lack a lot. That's why we need him to do lots of things for us.)"[216]

Marcos readily cedes supreme authority to others. He noted: "I have the honor to have as my superiors the best Tzeltal, Tzotzil, Chol, Tojolabal, Mam, and Zoque men and women. I have lived with them for more than 10 years and I am proud to obey them and serve them with my arms and my soul."[217] This indicates a sharp break from past guerrilla practices of caudillo-style leadership. As anthropologist Hernández Navarro, who has worked with coffee growers in Chiapas, commented, "Long before they took up arms, there was a tradition of collective decision-making."[218] This tradition dates back at least to the collectively led rebellion of 1712.[219]

Marcos commented further on decision-making: "Even the Clandestine Committees cannot make certain decisions, the most important decisions. They are limited to such a degree that the Clandestine Committees cannot decide which path the organization is going to follow until every compañero is consulted."[220] An obvious example of such grass-roots consultation was the decision on whether to accept the proposed peace accords drafted early in March 1994.

The EZLN relies on a mass base resulting from decades of organizing in the area. This gives it a very different character than other groups such as the 26th of July Movement which came from Mexico to Cuba on a boat in 1956 and immediately started fighting the dictator Fulgencio Batista. Such differences from Cuban and subsequent insurgencies led sociologist Rodolfo Stavenhagen to comment, "It is not a 1970s-style movement, a movement of a handful of visionaries."[221]

The EZLN communiqué of 6 January responded to the early vituperation directed against the EZLN. It stated that there was no foreign participation in or assistance to the EZLN nor any connection to armed groups in Central America or elsewhere. It also affirmed Mexican nationalism, noting EZLN tactics were based on a study of

Mexican military history. The same communiqué also responded to charges leveled at Bishop Ruiz and declared that the EZLN had no ties to the Catholic Church.

Marcos stated that arms for the movement were: 1) purchased in small lots, especially along the Texas-Mexico border, 2) seized from drug traffickers by the Mexican police and army and then sold to rebels rather than being turned in to higher authorities, 3) taken from cattlemen's hired gunmen, who are trained by the army and police, and 4) the mixed arms, such as shotguns, normally found among rural people. He supported his claim concerning traffickers as a source by noting that, according to government statistics, the number of traffickers apprehended was 10 times greater than the number of arms reported as confiscated. He concluded that this statistic either indicated unarmed traffickers or the seizure of arms which went unreported. Marcos also lamented the inability of the EZLN to find a good arms dealer. If it had, Marcos commented, the EZLN would have advanced to the Sierra de Ajusco on the southern edge of Mexico City.[222]

Once the offensive began, rebels seized many arms which had been stockpiled by local ranchers to prevent land take-overs by peasants. Marcos referred to such arms seizures as the EZLN's effort at gun control. The number of weapons stockpiled by ranchers is indicated by one single operation in 1992, when 400 well-armed cattlemen drove off land invaders. The arms most commonly taken from cattlemen were Chinese SKS automatic rifles, Uzi submachine guns, AK-47s, and automatic pistols. Rebels claimed they captured additional arms at Rancho Nuevo and at seized police stations.[223]

The most famous single EZLN weapon ironically proved to be a fake fake. Pictures were published worldwide, including in *Newsweek*, of a body identified as that of a slain Zapatista lying in the Ocosingo market alongside his fake wooden rifle. After photographers began comparing photos, they realized that the first to arrive on the scene had taken photos without the wooden rifle. Only in later pictures did the "rifle" appear. When the person in the photo was finally identified, it turned out that he was not a rebel, but an Ocosingo resident caught in the crossfire. No one ever determined who had placed the wooden rifle by his body.[224]

In its communiqué of 6 January, the EZLN specifically denied that it had resorted to kidnapping, robbery, or extortion to obtain money for arms. Cooper, however, noted that outside analysts had reported that a wave of kidnappings had netted the EZLN as much as $10 million.[225] Others suggested the use of agricultural loans to fund the rebellion.[226]

The EZLN rejected alliances with any of the Mexican presidential candidates. Rafael Aguilar Talamantes, president of the Cardenista Party of National Reconstruction (PFCRN), offered his party as a "peaceful arm" of the EZLN. The rebels declined the offer. Marcos, when asked in February which presidential candidate he preferred for the 1994 presidential elections, noted he had been instructed to avoid endorsing any party.[227] On another occasion, he flippantly referred to the PRI, the PRD, and the PAN, respectively, as the "Father, Son, and Holy Ghost."[228] In an interview, Mario commented: "We already voted for the PRI, and nothing happened; we already voted for the PAN, and nothing happened. And we voted for the PRD, and nothing happened."[229]

Zapatista rhetoric has concentrated on principles, such as democracy and justice, to the almost total exclusion of a program. In a document drafted in 1993 and made available on 1 January 1994, the EZLN offered its version of land reform. Its reform would take land holdings of more than 50 hectares of good land or 100 hectares of poor land to create co-operative farms for the landless. Very little was said about industry, although the proposed EZLN Labor Law stipulated that foreign firms would have to pay workers in Mexico the same amount as they paid employees outside Mexico.[230] This would lower the number of working poor, but would limit job creation—just the opposite of what Mexico needs.

Marcos commented on the EZLN's ideology:

> The directorate of our army has never spoken about Cuban or Soviet socialism. We have always spoken about the basic rights of the human: education, housing, health, food, land, good pay for our work, democracy. All of our thoughts about the workers and campesinos and the revolution are taken from the Mexican revolutionary heroes Flores Magón, Pancho Villa, and Emiliano Zapata. Their ideas and hopes of liberty are our inspiration. Some may call this socialism. But it doesn't matter what name you give these demands. In Mexico, there is no democracy. It doesn't matter what you think. Only

> the political goal of the government party wins—*always* wins. We say, make a democratic space, make enough liberty so that we can decide which leaders we agree with—and by "we," I mean the people, not the Zapatista army.[231]

Bishop Ruiz also commented on EZLN ideology:

> Their ideology remains a mystery. It seems this doesn't bother them much. In their communiqués, they show a combination of nationalism and socialism. The fundamental goal of their struggle is solving concrete problems which have the common thread of justice for the poor. Perhaps for this reason their message has had such a great impact and has been quickly understood. That's why the rebellion is felt to be on behalf of those excluded from the system—Indians and non-Indians.[232]

Author Jorge Castañeda characterized EZLN ideology as armed reformism. Rebels took up arms. However, they accepted the market as the guiding force in society. Castañeda commented that such an acceptance was "reluctant in some cases, more or less enthusiastic in others, but none the less it was real."[233]

Observations concerning the EZLN abound. Anthropologist Andrés Fábregas noted that the accomplishments of the EZLN were unique in that it had managed to unite the disparate ethnic and religious groups in the area.[234] Journalist Cooper praised the genius of calling for democracy rather than for the EZLN to seize power. If the EZLN had chosen the latter course, it would have raised others' fear of a new dictatorship.[235] Heberto Castillo, a 1988 presidential candidate, noted that no organization of the post-revolutionary period has accomplished so much as fast as the EZLN.[236] Finally, anthropologist Luis Hernández Navarro notes, "Clearly, they are not rebelling because they have been duped by anyone, but rather because they have chosen a path—a questionable one perhaps—in response to their perception of their dwindling prospects."[237]

Castañeda, however, notes that the rebels' ability to shape the destiny of Mexico as a nation is limited. He sees Mexico as too urban and too large for the EZLN to appeal to from its base in Chiapas. Also, he noted that the Mexican government is not in such ill repute as were the governments headed by Batista in Cuba and Somoza in Nicaragua, which permitted rebel triumphs there.[238]

Chapter 6: The United States Connection

> It's remarkable in a sense that someone, a president of the United States, who spoke about Mexico almost every day for a couple of months last year during the NAFTA debate, has managed not to say a word about Mexico, not to pronounce the word Mexico in public over the past month, given that the Chiapas uprising is arguably the most important political event in Mexico in 25 years.
>
> —Jorge Castañeda, 2 Feb. 1994[239]

The low-key response by the U. S. government to the rebellion was a sure sign of the passing of the Cold War. In early January, Christine Shelly, a State Department spokeswoman, said the department did not have enough information to make a general statement, but the "changes announced in the declaration of President Salinas indicate they are on the right course to solve the problem."[240]

Even though the *Washington Post* covered the rebellion extensively, it was only on 30 January that it had a feature on U.S. policy toward the Chiapas rebellion. This reflected the lack of public comment on the matter by the Clinton administration. Even though Chiapas is much closer than Bosnia, President Clinton found much more to say about problems there than about those in Chiapas. Apparently, Clinton, after so vigorously extolling Mexico's virtues during the NAFTA debate, was unwilling to call these same virtues into question.

The highest official from the executive branch quoted in the *Post* article was Alexander F. Watson, assistant secretary of state for inter-American affairs. Watson did his best to be even-handed. He noted,

"There's no doubt that events in Chiapas derive from poverty and lack of ability of the Mexican system—the government and everybody else—to deal with some of the fundamental problems in that part of the world." He then proceeded to compliment Salinas, noting: "I'm encouraged that President Salinas has picked two first-rate people like [Interior Secretary Jorge] Carpizo and [Peace Commissioner Manuel] Camacho to work on this. ... I think the Mexicans are heading in the right direction."[241]

While members of the executive branch went out of their way to avoid criticizing Salinas, some members of the legislative branch had no such reservations. It is, however, unclear whether they did so out of concern for human rights or to continue the battle waged over NAFTA. The same Congress members who had opposed NAFTA spearheaded the legislative response to the uprising.

On 20 January, some U.S. Congress members who had opposed NAFTA wrote Salinas asking him to investigate human-rights abuses in Chiapas. They organized a delegation, including Rep. Joe Kennedy, D.-Mass., to travel to Chiapas and investigate. Early in February, Congressman Robert Torricelli, D.-N.J., called hearings on Chiapas in the Western Hemisphere Subcommittee of the Foreign Relations Committee, over which he presides.

At the hearings, Watson again showed extreme reluctance to admit that NAFTA might have a negative impact on some Mexicans. Rather, he stated that the rebellion showed how important NAFTA was, since it was key to a strong Mexican economy, which would provide Mexico with needed jobs.

John Shattuck, assistant secretary of state for human rights, was more critical. He noted, "The military denies responsibility for abuses, even in cases where there were multiple witnesses of public beatings and of persons verified to have been taken into military custody."[242]

The only publicly revealed U.S. support to the Mexican military was the sale of 420,000 field rations (MREs) for $3.1 million. It is highly questionable if further military aid would have benefited the Mexican government, since the specter of the Mexican government's using U.S.-supplied weapons to combat peasants fighting in the name of Mexican nationalism would be a gross affront to many.[243]

The rebels accused the United States of indirectly aiding the government by tolerating the use of U.S.-supplied helicopters and communications equipment to fight the Zapatistas. A 13 January EZLN communiqué declared:

> We ask whether the U.S. people and their Congress approved this military and economic aid to fight drug traffickers or to murder Indians in southeastern Mexico. Troops, airplanes, helicopters, radars, communication equipment, arms, and military paraphernalia are now being used, not to fight drug traffickers and the main *capos* of the drug Mafia, but to repress the just struggles of the Mexican people and of the Chiapan Indians in the southeastern part of our country, and to kill innocent men, women, and children.[244]

James Jones, U.S. ambassador to Mexico, partially corroborated the Zapatista charges. He noted that military equipment supplied to combat traffickers had in fact been employed in Chiapas. However, he exonerated Mexicans of wrong-doing. He stated that, since the Mexican government had assured him the equipment was only used logistically in Chiapas, rather than in combat against the EZLN, its use was not in violation of the terms under which it was supplied.[245] Journalist John Ross differed, noting that the Mexican government deployed at least three Bell 212 helicopters to provide logistical support for the army counterattack against the EZLN.[246] Similarly, Marcos named four municipalities—San Cristóbal, Ocosingo, Altamirano, and Las Margaritas—where he said rebels had seen U.S.-supplied helicopters fighting against them.[247]

Human Rights Watch/Americas faulted the absence of any expression of human-rights concern by the Clinton administration during the early days of the uprising, at a time when such comments might have helped minimize abuse. Even when given a ready-made opportunity, such as Secretary of State Warren Christopher's 9 January appearance on "This Week with David Brinkley," the administration failed to act. Despite independent human-rights groups having already reported abuses, Christopher merely stated, "Governments do have to take steps in order to protect law and order."[248]

Human Rights Watch/Americas also noted that the U.S. embassy in Mexico City announced on 3 January that it had dispatched a five-member team to Chiapas the previous day. The State Department in Washington later dodged questions concerning human rights in

Chiapas, claiming it had no independent way of knowing what was happening there.[249]

John Maggs of the *Journal of Commerce* feels that the Clinton administration is simply continuing the Mexico policy inherited from the Bush administration. He characterized that policy as a belief that economic integration will act as an "invisible hand" pushing Mexico to democracy and improved human rights.[250]

Chapter 7: After the Cease-fire

> The guerrillas have given violent expression to the discontent felt by many Mexicans who have yet to enjoy the benefits of change.
>
> The *Economist* [251]

Unlike even the debate preceding the NAFTA vote, the Chiapas uprising caused Mexicans to re-evaluate the direction in which their country was moving. PRD leader Heberto Castillo noted, "The millions of dollars spent to promote Salinas went down the drain."[252] Historian Lorenzo Meyer compared the Chiapas revolt to the Revolution against Porfirio Díaz: "During the Díaz administration, as now, the preservation of authoritarian power was based less on repression than on acceptance of the inevitability and invincibility of the president's modernizing plans." Meyer also noted that violent protests against modernization broke out just as each regime was patting itself on the back. Díaz was celebrating the 100th anniversary of the start of the independence struggle. Salinas was celebrating the passage of the North American Free Trade Agreement.[253]

Meyer also noted that both the Díaz and Salinas regimes responded to challenges to their power by reshuffling their cabinets. On 10 January 1994, Salinas removed Interior Secretary González Garrido. His record of human-rights abuse and rigged elections when he was governor of Chiapas became an embarrassment after the uprising led to media scrutiny of him. Rather than offering the usual flattery about an outgoing official's years of meritorious service, Salinas merely stated, "This morning I accepted the resignation of Patrocinio González Garrido."[254] Salinas was not in a reflective mood at the time. He simply commented that González Garrido's removal was in response to "that which didn't work."[255]

González Garrido's replacement was Jorge Carpizo, the former head of the National Commission for Human Rights, who at the time of González Garrido's removal was serving as attorney general. Carpizo was one of the few in the cabinet who had the image of believing in the rule of law.

On 18 January, Elmar Setzer, who had succeeded González Garrido as governor of Chiapas, was replaced. The Chiapas legislature voted by secret ballot to replace him with Javier López Moreno. After the voting, each ballot was read aloud. The PRI legislators all voted for López Moreno. When the lone opposition vote, cast by PRD member Jack Demóstenes Muñoz, was read as being for Marcos, applause broke out.[256]

The choice of López Moreno led many to question the PRI's acceptance of reform, even after the uprising. López Moreno had been state secretary of education under Castellanos Domínguez. This led many to feel that he was tainted politically. His selection of several individuals who had served in the Castellanos Domínguez administration to serve in his government also caused concern.[257]

Government spending sharply increased after the Zapatista rebellion. This could have been in response to the uprising, or it could have been the normal increase in government spending during an election year. In any case, on 10 February, Salinas announced a 10-point, $350 million program for 260,000 small coffee producers. The program offered health benefits, training, credit, and assistance in processing their crop.[258] That same week, the government announced a 78 percent increase in rural spending, of which 55 percent would be for social projects.[259] On 2 March, 2,600 new Solidarity projects, with a budget of $235 million, were announced.[260] Silviano Herrera Ortiz, leader of the combative Oaxacan Teachers' Union, commented: "They said because of the 1 January uprising, they have instructions 'from above' to attend to the demands of our communities."[261]

Many Chiapans not involved in actual combat were affected by the rebellion. As many as 50,000 people fled the war zone due to fear of being involved in combat or due to loss of their source of livelihood. Thirty-seven shelters were set up for them in 13 localities. Some Mexicans took refuge in Huehuetenango, Guatemala, reversing the direction of recent refugee flow. Those displaced put a severe

The Displaced, Las Margaritas *Paulina Hermosillo*

strain on the already meager social safety net in Chiapas. Their plight was eased somewhat by massive shipments of relief supplies from other areas of Mexico.[262]

Marcos charged that deliberate efforts were made to drive residents from their homes. He declared:

> Groups of cattlemen and their private gunmen, the organized cattlemen of Ocosingo, Altamirano, and Las Margaritas, enter communities, saying: "The Zapatistas are coming. We'll give $3 to anyone who wants to leave." People become frightened. Those who are familiar with the Zapatistas do not share this fear. They say: "Here comes the army. We're going to be bombed." Then they become afraid and flee. They grab their things, their coffee, and their cattle. The cattlemen then say, "Don't take them," and they buy the cattle. However, they don't pay the $300 a cow might cost, but only $3 to $30.[263]

Even though there was little physical damage from the fighting, the effect of the rebellion rippled through the economy of Chiapas. Three oil exploration companies halted work in the Lacandón, laying off at least 1,500 workers. The government-owned company Pemex suspended oil drilling in the area. Five hundred workers from the Compañía Mexicana de Geofísica had to hike out in January when food quit arriving. They only learned of the rebellion when they reached populated areas.[264] Commercial activity in the state's 25,000 shops declined about 50 percent compared to 1993, forcing several to close. Tourism, a major industry, was hit hard. Hotel occupancy was down to five percent in January and February.[265] An early estimate predicted that 80 percent of the 1994 coffee crop would be lost since the Guatemalans who usually pick the crop could not enter Mexico.[266] Even if coffee was picked, many producers were unable to ship it to market. Other Chiapans complained that Mexican army soldiers manning check points would not allow them to take goods to market and that soldiers stole goods from them on their return, charging they were trying to supply the rebels.[267]

The rebellion had an economic impact at the national level. The Mexican stock market, or *bolsa*, had climbed 94 percent in 1993. However, on 3 January, the first day of trading after the rebellion, it lost 3.86 percent. A week later, it dropped another 6.3 percent in one day. The market then responded favorably to news that peace talks would begin and started to rise again.

The presidential campaign of PRI candidate Luis Colosio was transformed. In a normal election year, attention would be focused on the PRI presidential candidate. When he was selected, Colosio was referred to, even in Spanish-language journals, as "Mr. Continuity." After the rebellion and the upwelling of popular support for the rebels, Colosio was forced to change directions in midstream without appearing to bite the hand that fed—or more accurately, chose—him. In Puebla, he declared, "We no longer want decisions imposed from the capital on communities, something which is often done in an authoritarian manner."[268] On the campaign trail, crowds, rather than accepting the usual promises, would respond with the same demands the EZLN had made in Chiapas. For example, when Colosio visited Guelatao, Oaxaca, indigenous people demanded judicial and cultural autonomy.[269]

Colosio's eclipse by events in Chiapas led to rumors that he would be dropped as the PRI's candidate. Speculation was so rife that Salinas was forced to publicly tell PRI officials not to "get tied up in knots *(no se hagan bolas)*" about replacing Colosio with another candidate.[270] Colosio's eclipse was so complete that author Romero Jacobo declared, "Colosio is, in political terms, one of the first victims of the EZLN."[271]

Camacho Solís, as peace negotiator, and former presidential aspirant passed over by Salinas the previous fall, again emerged as a possible presidential contender. Some saw him as a substitute PRI candidate, others as a candidate of an opposition party. A committee was even formed in Guerrero to promote his candidacy.[272] Rumors of Camacho Solís' candidacy only faded when he formally announced he would not be a candidate. He later explained his decision not to seek the presidency: "The situation was very precarious. I had to make it very clear that I was not using the negotiations as a steppingstone to the presidency. I placed peace in Chiapas ahead of my presidential ambitions."[273]

The Mexican newsmagazine *Proceso* provides a good indication of how the Chiapas story crowded out the presidential campaign early in 1994.

		Pages of Chiapas coverage	Pages of presidential campaign coverage
Issue dated	Jan. 10	70	1
	Jan. 17	39	4
	Jan. 24	53	1
	Jan. 31	28	8
	Feb. 7	37	5
	Feb. 14	24	0
	Feb. 21	40	8
	Feb. 28	41	2
	March 7	39	5

The rebel spokesman, Subcommander Marcos, also contributed to the eclipsing of Colosio. Marcos became such a familiar figure that he was sometimes referred to in the press simply as "*El Sub*." He carefully cultivated an image, wearing a black ski mask and a bandolier of red shotgun cartridges over a waterproof jacket and a thick black pancho. His celebrity status was described as

"Marcosmania."[274] Many acres of trees were felled to print speculation as to Marcos' true identity. Journalists seized on hints that he dropped concerning his identity, even though he declared, "The only sure thing about what I have said about my identity is that it's false—mere repartee with the press."[275]

Marcos very effectively kept media attention focused on Chiapas with his widely quoted sound bites. At the start of negotiations, he commented, "Why is it necessary to kill and die to get anyone to pay any attention to us?" When asked why he wore a mask, he responded he did not have anything to hide, not even any parking tickets. Guillermoprieto commented that Marcos was "more articulate, cosmopolitan, humorous, and coquetishly manipulative than any guerrilla leader of El Salvador or Nicaragua who ever locked horns with the press."[276]

Other rebel actions were effectively staged for the media. Almost 300 reporters were taken in 40 chartered minibuses to watch the release of kidnapped former Gov. Castellanos Domínguez. Rebels had put the former governor on trial and given him a life sentence "doing manual labor in an indigenous community of Chiapas and thus earning food and the necessities for survival." They then pardoned him, noting he would have "to live for the rest of his life with the hurt and shame of having been pardoned by those whom he had humiliated, kidnapped, dispossessed, robbed, and murdered for so long."[277]

At the release ceremony, transmitted live on TV and in front of the assembled press corps, charges were read of Castellanos Domínguez's past actions, including murder, unjustified arrest, expulsion of residents, illicit enrichment, and violation of human rights. A rebel spokesman read a detailed list of Castellanos Domínguez's 10 estates whose total area was 20,800 hectares (26 times the area allowed by the land-reform law).[278]

In mid-January, 675 outstanding figures in Mexican culture and politics, many of whom represented civic groups, released a statement. It noted that the PRI had justified its existence with the claim that at least it could keep the peace. The statement concluded that this rationale was no longer valid, and that "the rebellion in Chiapas, highly local, rural, and racial, is a sign of advanced social decomposition and national policy disarray. ... It indicates electoral fraud and the lack of liberty and democracy. Such manipulation could cause the Chiapas rebellion to extend throughout the country."[279]

To overcome the negative publicity from the rebellion and rebels' criticism of Mexican elections, eight political parties, including the PAN, the PRI, and the PRD, signed an agreement. The agreement called for a halt to giving government funds to a favored political party, for an independent prosecutor to investigate election fraud, for fair treatment for all parties in the news media, and for an independent body to rule on the fairness of elections.[280] Alan Riding, author of the book *Distant Neighbors*, commented that the rebels "had thrown the entire political system into disarray and given Mexico a hefty shove toward becoming a real democracy."[281]

The rebellion led to other copy-cat actions in Chiapas. Ten city halls were occupied, not by EZLN members, but by citizens fed up with corrupt officials. In Teopisca, protesters occupied the city hall in their efforts to remove Mayor Héctor Álvarez Gordillo for pocketing government money. His removal came after women tied up two federal deputies and then began to negotiate by phone with the governor for his removal.[282] Miguel Hernández, a corn farmer in Teopisca, declared: "By grace, the Zapatistas have opened our eyes. We do not know them, but we must thank them. Before, we did not have the valor to do this."[283] Although those occupying the city hall in Teopisca did not use guns, some of their backers did have guns, which they used to shoot out the tires of an official's car when he tried to run a roadblock they had set up. The protesters later commented that they did not like violence, but if the Zapatistas could get results through the use of violence, protesters in Teopisca would resort to violence, too.[284]

In Cintalapa, 2,500 peasants from 41 communities blocked the offices of three banks, demanding that past crop loans be written off. They noted that prices had fallen for all of their cash crops—cacao, corn, soy, and cattle.[285] Other protesters' demands included increased agricultural credit, cheaper fuel, tax exemptions, and electrification.[286]

The rebellion loosened old inhibitions and removed the possibility of immediate retribution. Individuals began to take land matters into their own hands. Numerous peasant groups simply moved onto lands they claimed, and remained. In Chilón, 2,000 Tzeltal Indians associated with the *Central Campesino Cardenista* occupied lands in the municipality, declaring that they had spent more than 20 years attempting to gain the land via the means provided for in the land-reform law. The Chilón Cattlemen's Association claimed that each of the properties taken had been legally certified as being below the maximum legally allowable size. The occupiers of the land responded by accusing ranchers of bribing land-reform officials to get their certifications.[287] By the beginning of March, more than 30,000 hectares of land in Chiapas had been occupied. Some of the occupiers had land claims dating back to 1744.[288]

In response to the emboldenment of the dispossessed in Chiapas, the wealthy, especially cattlemen, organized in opposition to land seizures and EZLN demands. Prior to the rebellion, these cattlemen, sometimes referred to as Chiapan contras, were part of an association which included 12,000 members in 60 local organizations.[289] The most prominent newly formed organization is the Citizens' Front for the Defense of the Dignity of San Cristóbal. It opposed the use of the Cathedral in San Cristóbal for peace negotiations and demanded the closure of the local newspaper *Tiempo*, the removal of those who had seized lands, and the expulsion of Bishop Ruiz. Cattlemen staged a demonstration in front of the state capital. They held signs which demanded that EZLN members be jailed and which denounced Bishop Ruiz, the "lying press," and leftist political parties.[290]

Some of the backlash smacked of paranoia. In Altamirano, protesters demanded the removal of 10 Dominican nuns. The nuns work as nurses at a charity hospital which mainly serves Indians. As many as 70 demonstrators gathered outside the hospital and shouted threats at the nuns. Local rancher Alfredo Kanter Solórzano declared: "The sisters are the ones who caused this entire situation. If the nuns do not leave, we will take our own measures."[291]

In January, the government employed its traditional divide-and-conquer tactics. It supported 280 peasant groups as they organized to form the State Council of Indigenous and Peasant Organizations (CEOIC). This was intended to limit support for the EZLN. The failure of this tactic became apparent when President Salinas attended a CEOIC meeting in Tuxtla Gutiérrez, at which the council presented a long list of grievances and stated publicly that it supported the EZLN.[292] It also called on national and international public opinion "to prevent the CEOIC from becoming just one more instrument of control that the state and federal governments use to

Nurses at hospital in Altamirano *Paulina Hermosillo*

prevent groups from addressing the real causes of the social, political, and military violence which affect Chiapas and the nation."[293]

The impact of the rebellion extended far beyond Chiapas, since, as political scientist Arturo Gómez noted, the rebels "have found widespread sympathy in Mexico and abroad—not for the war, necessarily, but for the justice of their case, and for the passionate demand to break with 500 years of oppression."[294]

Following the uprising, groups throughout Mexico began to raise demands similar to those raised by the Zapatistas. The Third Congress of Indigenous Communities of Michoacán denounced the changes to Article 27, demanded 40 congressional seats for indigenous people and autonomy for indigenous areas and offered support for the EZLN.[295] A group of Mixtec Indians in Puebla formed the Zapatista Movement of the South and declared, "We're fed up with misery, exploitation, discrimination, hunger, corrupt officials, and of being second-class Mexican citizens, just like our Chiapan brothers and sisters are."[296] Sugar cane-cutters in Michoacán, and other groups in Puebla, Oaxaca, Querétaro,

Coahuila, and Chihuahua, made similar demands and threatened to take up arms if these demands were not met.[297]

Support was not confined to rural areas. On 12 January, 100,000 marched in a Mexico City demonstration. Although originally billed as a peace demonstration, Salinas' cease-fire declaration earlier that day turned it into more of a pro-EZLN demonstration. Marchers chanted, "*Zapata vive-vive, la lucha sigue-sigue* (Zapata lives, the struggle continues)." The main speaker at the post-march rally was Dominican priest Miguel Concha. He declared: "We all fervently desire peace, but not a peace at any price. Our goal is a true peace based on justice for all and respect for and recognition of everyone's rights." Concha also called for the recognition of the EZLN and dialogue between the government and the rebels. Finally, he warned of the consequences of continuing with the current economic development model.[298]

Marcos commented that an immediate change produced by the rebellion was that "whites" [his term] were respecting Indians in Chiapas for the first time because they see them with guns.[299]

Even though the uprising harmed many economically, it also created some small niche markets. Street vendors did a thriving business peddling buttons, T-shirts, dolls, and even condoms with Marcos' picture on them.

Chapter 8: Negotiations

> The rebels want their demands be attended to for once and for all. They want all the marginal sectors to be able to participate effectively in society. Above all, they want a total reform of the social and political system, which until now has been dominated by the absolute control of the official party.
>
> — Bishop Samuel Ruiz, 15 Feb. 1994[300]

In a 10 January communiqué, the EZLN announced the conditions it demanded the government meet before dialogue could begin. They were: 1) recognition the EZLN as a belligerent force, 2) a cease-fire and the return of troops in Chiapas to barracks in other parts of Mexico, and 3) the withdrawal of federal troops from rebel territory.[301]

President Salinas' appointment of Manuel Camacho Solís as negotiator was widely seen as a step towards peace. As mayor of Mexico City, Camacho Solís had proved willing to negotiate disputes rather than use brute force, as some members of the Salinas administration did. On 18 January, the rebels commented on the efforts of Camacho Solís and Bishop Ruiz: "We welcome their efforts and reiterate our willingness to listen and keep open all possible channels of communication for the well-being of our people and of the whole nation."[302]

Camacho Solís responded in an equally conciliatory manner on 29 January, noting, "The conditions exist which permit a political solution which will lead to a dignified peace for everyone." He also commented that a vital element of such a solution would be "progress toward democracy."[303]

Despite hopes for an early start of negotiations, weeks passed before the talks finally began. Each side engaged in verbal sparring. In a 4 February communiqué, rebels noted: "The CCRI-CG of the EZLN will go to the negotiating table with reservations because of its lack of confidence in the federal government. They want to buy us with a ton of promises." Time-consuming delays included providing for the security of rebel negotiators and accommodating the hundreds of journalists accredited for the negotiations.

The negotiating process raised a number of extremely complex issues. One was with whom should the government negotiate. In addition to the EZLN, there are numerous other peasant and indigenous groups in Chiapas which also have opinions. And of course the cattlemen have their views. Questions also arose concerning Camacho Solís' power. Could he sign away a 1,000-hectare estate or re-write an election law on his own? If he could not, who could make a concrete offer to the rebels? Finally, could the negotiators make changes at the national level, such as repealing the changes to Article 27, or only act on issues relating to Chiapas?

The government's brushing these issues aside reflected its desire to get started, since peasant grievances were pouring in from other states and rebels were winning the propaganda war they were waging in the media. Also, the government had little maneuvering room since the world situation made military solutions unacceptable. As the *Economist* noted, "Unless it brought instant success, real toughness would these days play badly in Washington and with foreign investors."[304]

It was finally agreed that negotiations, officially known as Meetings of Peace and Reconciliation (*Jornadas por la Paz and la Reconciliación*), would be held in the Cathedral of San Cristóbal. To provide security, there were three human rings around the Cathedral. One was composed of 300 individuals from non-governmental organizations, one by 500 military policemen without firearms, and a third by 400 members of the Mexican Red Cross.[305] A rebel demand was that the TV network Televisa be banned from covering the negotiations. This network has often been accused of biased coverage and its headquarters has been the site of repeated demonstrations organized by dissident groups protesting slanted news coverage.

Security rings around Cathedral *Paulina Hermosillo*

Crowds applauded the appearance of Marcos and the rebel negotiators. The rebel delegation was made of 19 Indian men and women, with Marcos serving as spokesman. They began by introducing themselves in sometimes broken Spanish or their native Tzeltal, Tzotzil, Chol, or Tojolabal. They each stated their name, their ethnic group, and affirmed being "100 percent Chiapan." Several wore traditional, colorful Indian dress characteristic of their community. All wore dark ski masks.

At the opening of negotiations on 22 February, government negotiator Camacho Solís said, "The successful outcome will be based on improved treatment for Mexico's Indian communities and on a commitment to democracy." He also noted: "Many of us want change in this country. We want more democracy. We want freedom. We want to make Mexico more just. The complex and difficult part is carrying this out, given Mexico's current national and international situation."[306]

In the amazingly short period of 10 days, a tentative accord was reached. Given the complexity of the issues, it was clear that many of the points were only guidelines which could be spelled out in detail later. Both sides agreed that the initial peace proposals would be taken back to the communities forming the rebels' base for discussion. There the accords would be ratified or rejected.

The accord was in the form of 34 rebel demands, with an official response to each demand:

- Demand 1: *Free and democratic elections.*

  This demand will be fulfilled by legislative changes enacted by the national congress.

- Demand 2: *The resignation of President Salinas and of governors who were fraudulently elected.*

  This demand will not be granted, although problems of election fraud will be addressed in a special congressional session on political reform.

- Demand 3: *Recognition of the EZLN as a belligerent force.*

  Although the EZLN will not be officially recognized as a belligerent force, it will be promised full guarantees and the right to decide on its future political and social role.

- Demand 4: *National re-organization to end highly centralized government administration.*

  The government will send to congress legislation providing political, economic, and cultural autonomy to Indian communities.

- Demand 5: *Election reform in Chiapas.*

  The state election law will be modified so that gubernatorial, legislative, and mayoral elections will be held on the same day.

- Demand 6: *Redirection of the electricity generated in Chiapas to communities in the state, and local investment of income from the sale of Chiapan oil.*

  The government will double the rate of electrification in rural areas.

- Demand 7: *Revision of NAFTA, given its negative impact on Indian communities.*

The Commerce Ministry will study the impact of NAFTA on Chiapas and, especially, on Indian communities.

- Demand 8: *Subdivision of large estates and repeal of recent changes in Article 27.*

  Legislation will be drafted for the subdivision of large estates, if it is in the "public interest," and for the protection of family lands in Indian communities.

- Demand 9: *Building and staffing hospitals.*

  Existing hospitals will be upgraded and personnel and medical facilities will be provided in areas lacking medical service.

- Demand 10: *An independent Indian radio station.*

  An independent station, run by Indians, will be licensed.

- Demand 11: *Rural housing.*

  Solidarity will draft a rural-housing program within 90 days, and construction will begin in the second half of 1994.

- Demand 12: *Ending illiteracy and improving schools.*

  Plans for improved education, with emphasis on bilingual education, will be drafted and implemented in September 1994.

- Demand 13: *Indian languages should be compulsory for primary through university education.*

  Bilingual education will be mandated in the state education law.

- Demand 14: *Respect for Indian culture and tradition.*

  This will be provided for in the General Law of the Rights of Indian Communities.

- Demand 15: *Ending discrimination against Indians.*

  Discrimination against Indians will be criminalized.

- Demand 16: *Indian autonomy.*

  New municipalities will be created and new laws passed to provide autonomy.

- Demand 17: *Administration of their own courts by Indian towns.*

  The state constitution and legal code will be modified to meet this demand.

- Demand 18: *Dignified jobs and just wages, along with enforcement of Federal Labor Law.*

  Job creation will be stimulated with support for agro-industry, marketing, infrastructure, and artisan production. Legal protection will be strengthened.

- Demand 19: *Fair prices for crops.*

  Bean and corn production will be supported by an existing government program, PROCAMPO, and coffee production will be supported with the already announced program.

- Demand 20: *Putting a stop to the plundering of Mexico's wealth, and above all, to the plundering of the wealth of Chiapas, where there is hunger and misery.*

  Strengthened local governments will be able to protect local wealth, since they will exercise control over those who exploit it.

- Demand 21: *Annulment of debts which cannot be paid by those in poverty.*

  The Treasury Ministry will evaluate the problem and propose a solution.

- Demand 22: *Ending hunger and malnutrition, establishing cooperative stores in each rural community, providing co-ops with trucks, and guaranteeing free government-supplied food for all children younger than 14.*

  Under UNICEF guidelines, within 60 days, the government and non-governmental organizations will began a nutrition program for children ages 0 to 6.

- Demand 23: *Immediate freedom for all political prisoners in Chiapas.*

The announced amnesty law will be applied, and other cases will be exhaustively reviewed.

- Demand 24: *A stop to army and police entry into rural areas, since they only come to repress and rob. A return to the Swiss government of Pilatus aircraft, used to bomb Indian towns, and a return to the U.S. government of helicopters supplied to the Mexican government.*

  A new law for Indian communities and new municipal governments will guarantee respect for the legal order.

- Demand 25: *Indemnification by the federal government of those suffering losses due to aerial bombardment or actions of the Mexican army.*

  Monetary support will be provided to victims of the uprising, including widows and orphans.

- Demand 26: *Permitting Indians to live in peace and tranquillity.*

  Provisions in this accord will allow this.

- Demand 27: *Repeal of the state penal code.*

  The state penal code will be revised.

- Demand 28: *Criminalizing expulsion from communities by government-backed caciques, and allowing the return of those expelled.*

  Expulsion will be made a crime.

- Demand 29: *Maternity clinics, day-care centers, nutritious food, kitchens, dining facilities,* nixtamal *and tortilla mills, and training programs for Indian women.*

  Support will be provided for women's demands to improve conditions in their homes, on the job, and in their communities.

- Demand 30: *Criminal trials of former governors Patrocinio González Garrido, Absalón Castellanos Domínguez, and Elmar Setzer.*

  These accords should reduce tension, which generates animosity.

- Demand 31: *Guarantees of safety for participants in the EZLN.*

  The amnesty prevents reprisals or criminal charges against EZLN members or its supporters.

- Demand 32: *Independence of human-rights groups.*

  The government's National Commission for Human Rights already serves to protect human rights, and increased activity by citizens and non-governmental organizations will guarantee further protection.

- Demand 33: *Creation of a non-partisan National Commission for Peace with Justice and Dignity.*

  Such a commission will be created.

- Demand 34: *Channeling through authentic representatives of Indian communities the aid to victims of the conflict.*

  The government and non-governmental organizations will guarantee this.[307]

In part, the speed with which the accords were drafted reflects the listing of mutually acceptable good intentions without specifying details. It also reflects the dedication of the negotiators. As Camacho Solís noted: "We put in 18-hour days. There were long waits without responses within the Cathedral. We were constantly afraid that, if what we were doing did not bear fruit, war would break out again and many would be killed."[308]

Camacho Solís commented after the negotiations were concluded:

> The agreements with the government will not resolve the problems of Chiapas merely by announcing funding. What will be necessary will be a change of attitudes, of reforms, and profound changes in the state. Such changes are the *sine qua non* to the creation of peace.[309]

President Salinas was more upbeat. He declared: "It is truly encouraging that the negotiations in Chiapas have produced notable, positive results. The list of demands has been responded to by carefully considering and meeting the Indians' demands for justice, well-being, and dignity."[310]

Not surprisingly, PAN presidential candidate Fernández de Cevallos was less enthusiastic. He noted, "The promises and commitments are of such a magnitude that they clearly cannot be met. ... I lament the abuses of the judicial and legislative process. ... The government only listens to society if it is pressured. Otherwise, it is blind and deaf to popular demands."[311]

The general consensus was that the proposed accords would be accepted by the rebels' base. In fact, most observers felt that the rebels, given their military weakness compared to the government, had been lucky to receive as favorable a settlement as they did.

Chapter 9: After the Negotiations

As was previously agreed, the EZLN negotiating team returned to rebel-controlled territory to discuss the proposed accords. They faced a daunting task, since there were more than 1,000 communities to be consulted. Merely getting the accords into understandable form was a challenge, since the proposals had to be translated into the major Indian languages of the area—Tzeltal, Tzotzil, Chol, and Tojolabal. Much of the terminology in the original Spanish version is simply lacking in these languages.[312]

During the time they were reviewing the proposals, the rebels emphasized that they would keep their guns. Marcos commented, "It seems like the government's game is to get out of the military conflict with a promise and move on to the elections without any pressure."[313]

After the government response to the EZLN demands was announced, there was a backlash from Chiapan businessmen, merchants, and politicians who claimed that Camacho Solís gave away too much. They staged marches and rallies at which they declared that he had violated the sovereignty of the state, especially in agreeing to change the state electoral calendar.

On 7 March, roughly 2,000 San Cristóbal residents met and demanded: 1) the Cathedral no longer be used for peace negotiations, 2) an end to land takeovers, and 3) the expulsion of Bishop Ruiz. The protesters threatened to burn the bishop's residence if he did not leave. Many of these protesters were Catholics who felt betrayed by their Church. Ten church buildings in San Cristóbal were symbolically closed by placing seals across their doors. The seals read:

> Fellow Catholics: Beginning today, this church and all those of the city will remain closed until Bishop Samuel Ruiz leaves

> the city, Chiapas, and Mexico. He is responsible for land takeovers and war in the region. ... Pray and worship at home. God knows you are with Him and God is everywhere.

Columnist Sergio Sarmiento commented that these declarations showed "the complexity of the situation and that there are groups other than the EZLN which have rights and opinions."[314]

The assassination in Tijuana of PRI presidential candidate Luis Donaldo Colosio on 23 March turned Mexico's attention back to the north. Marcos commented that Colosio had advocated a political solution to problems in Chiapas. He also stated, "If there is a group within the government which will benefit from the assassination, it is the group which wants to drown in blood, not only the EZLN, but any attempt to democratize Mexico."[315]

Just after the assassination, the Clandestine Indian Revolutionary Committee (CCRI) suspended further consideration of the proposed accords. It charged that the air force had broken the cease-fire by bombing an area along the Comitán-Altamirano highway and that troop strength in Chiapas had doubled. This news led the rebels to declare that a government military offensive was imminent.[316]

Mobilization to commemorate the 75th anniversary of Zapata's death on 10 April indicated that the issues raised by the EZLN were still reverberating throughout Mexico. There were several marches in Chiapas that day, including one in the north Chiapas town of Palenque, in which 500 marched and painted public buildings with slogans praising the EZLN and Marcos.[317] In Mexico City, 50,000 gathered to honor Zapata. An EZLN communiqué was read to those assembled. It declared:

> The right to land for those who work it is inalienable, and the battle cry "land and liberty!" is still relevant today. Under the guise of neo-liberalism, a shadow has been cast upon our land. All the peasants who struggle for their rights are jailed and murdered. Salinas' reform of Article 27 of the Constitution is treasonous. The President, who usurped executive power, should be tried for this crime.[318]

In Chiapas, after the negotiations, there were killings, confrontations between peasant groups, land takeovers, plundering of property, expulsions of residents for political-religious motives, kidnappings, an increase in common crimes, the seizing of city halls, hunger strikes, and work stoppages. Unknown persons attacked a Mexican army roadblock, killing one soldier. The EZLN denied responsibility. Fifteen people were killed in land disputes during the first two weeks of April.[319]

In various parts of the state, peasants continued to appropriate (they say "recuperate") lands, including banana and coffee plantations. By June, peasants had occupied 100,000 hectares. Land owners in the north of the state blocked highways to bring attention to their plight.[320] Leonel Aguilar, a rancher from Ocosingo, commented: "If the government doesn't do anything, we will have to use weapons. We can hire at least 500 guns."[321]

The government responded to the land takeovers in several ways. In some instances, it distributed land to the landless. In the first five months of 1994, the state government distributed 25,000 hectares. Of that area, more than 8,700 hectares had previously been granted to peasants by presidential decree. More than 9,000 hectares were

Holy Week in Zapatista Territory, San Miguel, Ocosingo *Paulina Hermosillo*

previously owned by the government. Finally, 7,300 hectares were bought for the landless at a cost of $670 per hectare.[322]

The government also negotiated with the State Council of Indigenous and Peasant Organizations (CEOIC) to prevent future land takeovers. In April, the CEOIC agreed to end takeovers and the government promised to end evictions. Shortly afterward in Teopisca, four groups were evicted from occupied land. The CEOIC claimed this ended the agreement. Soon, 39 additional land takeovers occurred.[323]

By the end of May, cattlemen claimed to have lost more than $200 million as a result of land takeovers.[324] To compensate landowners for their losses, the government agreed to pay rent, retroactive to 1 January, for property which had been occupied by peasants in the area controlled by the rebels. During the first five months of the year, these payments totaled $5.2 million.[325]

This bailout was criticized by CIOAC member Jorge Arturo Luna, who noted that cattlemen were receiving seven times more per hectare than they had previously received from renting the same land to peasants. Luna also noted that it would be a much sounder policy to use the money as down payments on land. This would enable the landless to buy up sections of large estates and thus establish small farms. At the same time, he criticized state spending priorities in general, noting that while 70 percent of Chiapas' population is in the countryside, most state spending is in urban areas.[326]

Disputes continued to swirl around the state's PRI mayors. In late April, hundreds of men and women surrounded the city hall in Venustiano Carranza, demanding the ouster of Mayor Enrique Aguilar Martínez. He resigned a day later and wrote to the legislature, "I am resigning for personal reasons and because I feel it will serve the interests of the state in maintaining social stability."[327] Not all of the mayors ceded power so gracefully. Residents of Villa las Rosas staged three separate sit-ins in an attempt to force Mayor Aymer Cancino Ruiz from office for embezzlement. After the third unsuccessful sit-in, residents set the city hall on fire.[328] Between 1 January and 30 April 1994, 31 of Chiapas' 111 mayors were forced out of office.[329]

From January through May of 1994, the federal government spent $66 million in Chiapas, 129 percent more than during the same period in 1993.[330] During that period, $1.8 million in credits was allocated to the Rural Collective Interest Association (ARIC), the

EZLN's main rival for peasant loyalty.[331] The National Indian Institute (INI) announced that it planned to spend $6.7 million in Chiapas between May and November of 1994. The INI projects included electrification, potable water, and support for beekeepers, fishermen, and producers of corn, beans, chile peppers, potatoes, cabbage, and tomatoes.[332] The government also announced a massive health-care program which would provide services to communities, including those with a population of less than 100.[333] Political scientist Luis Javier Garrido characterized the government strategy in Chiapas as being one of "subduing the peasants in arms with an unquantifiable flood of material resources."[334]

The major story emerging from Chiapas in the two months after the Colosio assassination was the mid-May visit to rebel-held territory by Cuauhtémoc Cárdenas, the presidential candidate of the PRD. Initially, the rebellion was seen as a boost to Cárdenas' center-left candidacy, since it reaffirmed his critique of recent Mexican economic development. One commentator noted, "Cuauhtémoc Cárdenas' cause has undoubtedly been helped by the Chiapas crisis which has highlighted the negative aspects of the PRI's policies."[335]

After his poor showing in the nationally televised presidential candidates' debate on 12 May, Cárdenas needed something to reinvigorate his campaign. However, that is not what he found the following week when he visited EZLN territory. Cárdenas was cordially received. Some 500 Zapatista troops marched for him in formation, performing military drills and singing revolutionary anthems. While he was careful to avoid attacking Cárdenas personally, Marcos delivered a widely publicized attack on Cárdenas' party. The rebel spokesman noted: "We have watched with preoccupation while the PRD tends to repeat the vices that have plagued the party in power since its formation. PRD members who struggle for democracy in the public arena lie, hatch palace intrigues within the party, restrict decision-making to top officials, split along ideological lines, and are constantly settling old political scores." In another widely quoted remark, Marcos commented on the PRD's move to the political center: "Yesterday, it was on the left. Today it is in the center. Where will it be tomorrow?"[336]

Chapter 10: Rejection

> The decision of the EZLN to reject the accords and maintain the truce has created a situation in which anything can happen. It also means that if the elections are not credible, hostilities could break out again in Chiapas and violence could extend to other parts of Mexico.
>
> — Sergio Aguayo Quezada, 1994[337]

Peace negotiator Camacho Solís originally felt that negotiations would resume soon after the first negotiating session. In early March, he described the proposed agreement to the Mexican Congress and stated: "I will return to Chiapas when I have a response from the EZLN. I don't know when that will be, maybe next week."[338]

Subcommander Marcos was less optimistic. He commented, "The committee (CCRI) finds it problematic that the government is acting as if there were already a pact or agreement."[339]

Bishop Ruiz similarly emphasized that a final settlement was still distant. In mid-March, he commented: "At the conclusion of the first phase of the dialogue, I clearly stated that these were not agreements. Nevertheless, the media are getting all excited and treating the government proposals as if they were final accords."[340]

Then came the 23 March assassination of PRI presidential candidate Colosio. This changed the political situation in which the rebels found themselves. Soon after Colosio's assassination, Camacho Solís commented:

> If the EZLN fails to realize that things changed with [Colosio's] murder—that there is a conservative backlash in the country. If the Zapatistas believe that they can maintain

> their popularity even if they do not come back to the negotiations, they will lose a great deal of strength. In practical terms, if they consolidate what they have won so far they can go down in history as one of the most successful armed movements ever, but if they do not work out the political mathematics of this correctly they can lose a great deal of what they've already achieved.[341]

The assassination delayed the rebel response. Thinking that it might signal a military offensive by the government, the rebels quit considering the proposals and went on alert. Only on 22 April did consideration of the proposals resume. Then, in each town, hamlet, or cluster of homes, there were assemblies to discuss the 32 proposals.[342]

When the rebels' response finally came, it burst like a bombshell. The EZLN rejected the government offer, stating that 97.88 percent of its base had voted against accepting the negotiated package. The reason given was that the government failed to guarantee democracy, liberty, and justice for all Mexicans. Rather than continuing with further negotiations in Chiapas, the EZLN called for a national convention of all "patriotic forces," which would write a new Constitution and call for new elections.

In addition, the EZLN declared that it would maintain the cease-fire. Rebels also stated that they would reject aid from federal, state, and municipal governments. Finally, they expressed their gratitude to Camacho Solís for "his genuine effort in search of a political solution to the conflict" and to Bishop Ruiz for resisting the pressures and threats he had received while mediating the peace process.

The tone of the rebels was certainly not one of defeat, or even compromise. Rather, one of the four communiqués they issued on 10 June declared: "Our struggle continues. The Zapatista flag will continue to fly in the mountains of southeast Mexico and *we will not surrender.*"[343]

Camacho Solís responded to the EZLN rejection, emphasizing the positive. He noted: "For us, the main point was stopping the violence, which in the first days of the uprising caused many deaths, produced more than 25,000 refugees, and led to an 8 percent production decline in Chiapas. We also protected the reputation of the army and shifted the focus of attention from the executive's resigning to advancing democracy and meeting the rebels' just demands."[344] He also noted that the cease-fire in Chiapas had held and that new institutions were being established to resolve Chiapas' problems.

Camacho Solís also addressed the rebels' major point of contention—the failure to ensure democracy at the national level. He stated, "Democracy should be strengthened by means of government institutions, by the constitutional process of legal change, by Congress, the parties, the media, and, of course, there is an important role for Mexican civil society to play in the future."[345]

President Salinas responded to the rejection by ordering the secretary of national defense to maintain the cease-fire in Chiapas. Salinas also stated that all federal, state, and municipal aid programs offered to the EZLN would be carried out, despite the rebels' having rejected the proposed accords.[346]

The rejection set off another round of praise and criticism. Seven hundred delegates from the 280 organizations in the State Council of Indigenous and Peasant Organizations (CEOIC) unanimously supported the EZLN decision.[347] Similarly, the National Union of Agricultural Workers (UNTA) said the EZLN was justified in rejecting the proposed accords since PRI governments had in the past been "characterized by betrayal."[348]

Pundits were divided. Julio Moguel said the EZLN rejection was justified because of government actions in the months after the cease-fire. The government, he noted, was buying riot-control equipment. It had failed to consider changes in Article 27 (providing for land reform) and Article 4 (providing equality before the law) of the Mexican constitution. He also noted a continuation of dirty politics in Chiapas, including substantial funding for the EZLN's rival, the Rural Collective Interest Association (ARIC), and the selection of conservative cattleman Jorge Constantino Kanter and ARIC leader Lázaro Hernández as PRI deputy candidates.[349]

Others were less supportive of the decision. Columnist Mauricio Merino noted that the initial EZLN demands could not have been more just. However, he commented on the rejection of the proposed accords:

> Their demands are no longer for a just, lasting peace, but a government led by Zapatista revolutionaries. This proclamation wipes out with a stroke of the pen the institutional

> route to democracy that thousands of Mexicans are committed to—certainly many more than are members of the Zapatista army—through their participation in political parties, non-governmental organizations, media, trade unions, universities, etc.[350]

Columnist José de Jesús García claimed that "the reason the EZLN leaders rejected the proposals is that they wanted to continue to be political leaders." He also questioned the accuracy of the reported vote count, noting that no media were allowed to observe the voting.[351]

After the rebels declared they would reject aid from government agencies, the Chiapas state government announced that, in areas of Chiapas not controlled by the rebels, it would continue with projects offered in the proposed accords. Such projects included bringing electricity to 304 rural communities, building roads, introducing solar-produced electricity in isolated rural areas, constructing 158 potable water systems, and extending radio and telephone communication.[352] In addition, the government announced that the 1994 budget of Solidarity in Chiapas would be $192 million, up from the originally projected $133 million.[353]

PRI presidential candidate Ernesto Zedillo, who replaced the assassinated Colosio, commented on the rejection of the proposed accords: "We were sure that the negotiations had been a success. We were told that they were a success. Now we truly feel that they were a failure."[354] Three days later, Camacho Solís resigned as peace commissioner, charging that Zedillo's characterizing the negotiations as a "failure" precluded him from continuing his work as the government's peace negotiator.

After Camacho Solís' resignation, Zedillo commented on the former negotiator's charges: "Frankly, I don't know why he linked his resignation to my statement. I know that, days before the rejection of the accords by the EZLN, he had told several people that he planned to leave the commission in Chiapas and engage in other activities."[355]

Marcos, however, shared Camacho Solís' concerns:

> I think that Camacho Solís felt that he had no support, and thus would be unable to move forward, since the 'supposed'

future president of Mexico was undercutting him and discrediting him. If he would only have remained as a figurehead without support from the government or his party, it seems that resigning was the logical thing to do.[356]

Chapter 11: After the Rejection

Chiapans have yet to develop new ways of living together, and the old ones refuse to die.

—Miguel Ángel Granados Chapa, 1994[357]

After rejecting the proposed peace accords, the rebels remained in control of an area of Chiapas on the border with Guatemala. Journalist Alma Guillermoprieto described the region occupied by the rebels as "a land of hamlets without electricity or health clinics, without passable dirt roads, or even a place to buy anything to eat or drink."[358]

Before 1 January 1994, the number of confrontations over land had decreased due to repression, internal division, and organizational disarray among those demanding land.[359] As a result of the uprising, however, the land question once again polarized Chiapas. By September 1994, cattlemen claimed that 68,000 hectares had been occupied illegally outside the area controlled by the EZLN, and that another 98,850 hectares had been taken over inside the area controlled by the EZLN.[360] In a study of 125 of these occupations, the government found that, in 88 cases, local residents had failed to file a claim to the land they occupied. In 30 other cases, claims had been denied. Seven other cases involved pending claims.[361]

The State Council of Indigenous and Peasant Organizations (CEOIC), in contrast, reported that it had located 33 estates with land holdings in excess of the legal size limit. Many of these estates, ranging in size up to 6,000 hectares, were owned by families which had recently immigrated to Mexico or belonged to families of ex-governors of Chiapas or ex-presidents of Mexico. Others were simply registered in the names of front men. The CEOIC noted that many cattlemen refused to sell their land to peasants, even if they were paid in cash. The reason is that they have no deeds, since they had simply appropriated the land by force.[362]

The CEOIC urged the government to use powers still provided by Article 27 of the Constitution to expropriate occupied lands in the public interest. Gov. López Moreno refused, reiterating his administration's "firm decision to respect private property and the will of owners. Constitutional order does not admit exceptions."[363]

Despite such declarations, by the end of July, 89 property owners had declared a willingness to sell occupied land. These sales would provide 2,350 peasants with 11,910 hectares. The CEOIC found this pace far too slow.[364] During the seven months that provision was being made for 2,350 peasants, the state's population grew by 75,000, assuming a 4 percent rate of population growth.

A typical news story in the summer of 1994 began, "Hundreds of peasants, presumably members of the PRD, armed with machetes and clubs, took over four cattle ranches in Frontera Comalapa." While many conflicts involved big landowners and the dispossessed, there were many shades of gray in between. In one CIOAC takeover in Socoltenango, land invaders beat landowner Esteban Hernández before he could flee. He only owned five hectares.[365]

During one week in mid-June, three properties in Mazatán and one in Suchiate were taken over by CEOIC members. Such takeovers led Felipe Arizmendi Esquivel, the bishop of Tapachula, to comment, "If the land takeovers continue, Chiapas could fall into social chaos that will harm the pacification process which we are all interested in."[366]

The most publicized single takeover occurred at the Liquidámbar coffee estate in the municipality of Jaltenango La Paz. There, owner Hermann Schimpf Wedekind lived in luxury on a 2,000-hectare coffee plantation. The estate survived the Cárdenas administration (1934-1940) unscathed, in part due to its owner having destroyed the day laborers' union which was threatening his control.[367] In 1954, the estate was divided into 15 nominally separate units so no single part would exceed legal size limits. Agricultural workers taking over the estate found such luxuries as a swimming pool, Jacuzzi, gym, billiards tables, flower gardens, VCRs (complete with porn videos), and a landing strip.

The 700 families—Mexican and Guatemalan—who lived and worked on the estate shared a markedly different existence. They

Land takeover on Comitán-Las Margaritas Highway *Paulina Hermosillo*

lived in shacks with dirt floors. During the harvest, they were required to work from 5 a.m. to 8 p.m. The going wage for such work was $2.35 a day. Rather than receiving cash, workers were paid in chits which could only be redeemed at the estate-owned store. This store permitted the owner to recoup as profits much of the wages paid out. Observers were quick to point out that such company stores—or *tiendas de raya*—were one of the salient characteristics of pre-revolutionary Mexico. Those taking over the land vowed to keep the estate and form a 700-family co-op to run it.[368]

In addition to land takeovers, peasants engaged in other forms of protest. Beginning on 10 June, 500 CEOIC members began a sit-in in front of the state capital, demanding justice on land issues. After eight days, they left, claiming that their demands had been partially met.[369] Many highways were blocked to press grievances and extract money from passing motorists. For example, 400 Indians armed with machetes and clubs blocked the Ocosingo-Palenque highway and demanded "contributions" from those passing by. Federal Highway Police prudently declined to respond, noting that they had no written instructions from the Secretary of Communications and Transport.[370]

Cattlemen and other landowners responded to land takeovers and demonstrations with their own mobilizations. Landowners staged a sit-in at the state capital which lasted more than three months. They hoped to pressure the government to oust peasants from illegally taken land. The sit-in was accompanied by a hunger strike.[371] A group named the Coalition of Citizens Organizations of Chiapas demanded the "re-establishment of a state of law." This coalition organized a six-hour closure of some 3,000 hotels, restaurants, banks, shops, and gas stations throughout the state to protest the government's failure to enforce the law.[372] Landowners repeatedly threatened to take the law into their own hands. In September, a group known as the Broad Front to Defend the Land announced the organization of "vigilantes" to protect private landowners' property.[373]

Cattlemen pleaded the justice of their cause. José Luis Aguilar, the dispossessed owner of a 21-hectare ranch in Altamirano, lamented: "My house was destroyed. I can't go back. It's not fair. The Zapatistas have a just cause, but so do we." Cattleman Constantino Kanter invoked the general economic well-being of the state: "What Chiapas needs is investment from outside. But without guarantees of public safety, these investments won't happen. And without investment, production will be low. That only means more poverty, more unhappiness, and more instability."[374]

The government ineffectively tried to placate the cattlemen, without being willing to risk a frontal confrontation with armed peasants. As a result, neither side was satisfied. In late June 1994, pressured by the landowners' sit-in and hunger strike, Gov. López Moreno pledged to oust peasants from 300 plots they had taken over. The CEOIC described such actions as "fascist." Police began removing land occupiers early in July. However, such efforts were almost immediately suspended after peasants responded with gunfire, wounding six policemen.[375]

In September, squatter removal resumed in earnest. Four hundred and fifty police were successful in removing squatters from four of nine occupied banana plantations in Suchiate. More than 100 were arrested during the removal. However, before they could be taken away to jail, other peasants freed them. Four policemen were injured by thrown rocks.[376] On 19 and 20 September, 113 peasants were arrested as more than 400 police removed them from occupied land in five different municipalities. The response of José Ángel Morales López, one of those ousted, reflects the experience of many. He commented that he was on the land because he needed a place to live "and since we saw that the land wasn't being used, we organized and built our huts where we felt we wouldn't bother anybody. However, if the authorities say we have to leave, we'll leave peacefully."[377]

Mayors' offices continued to be targets. In El Bosque, some 200 peasants belonging to the Labor Party (PT) occupied the city hall and seized the mayor. He was kept tied up at the city hall as a hostage. The occupiers charged him with abuse of authority and embezzlement.[378] In Tuxtla Chico, peasants armed with clubs and machetes occupied the city hall to protest the arrest of 14 of their comrades when they were evicted from land they had occupied. Twelve employees were held hostage until those detained were released. Rather than admit wrong doing, the occupiers claimed the land was theirs, noting it had been awarded to them in 1943, but never transferred to them.[379]

While the government was irresolute on removing peasants from occupied lands, it wholeheartedly financed projects in an attempt to win Chiapans' hearts and minds. In July, an observer noted that, largely due to massive government spending, the rebellion "appears to be in full retreat." While rebels were surrounded by the Mexican army, spending for jobs, housing, social services, and infrastructure was concentrated in areas near but not in rebel-held territory. Many found the $7-a-day jobs on these projects attractive.[380]

The list of announced programs seemed to be the product of an inexhaustible cornucopia. They included:

- $88 million for federal health spending in 1994.[381]
- 4,302 classrooms rehabilitated and 2,365 new educational spaces built.[382]
- $846,766 provided to ARIC to support its members.[383]
- 113 potable water systems, benefiting 220,000 people.[384]
- Expanded INI nutritional programs for children younger than 5, pregnant women, and nursing women.[385]
- Five hospitals being built, restored, or enlarged.[386]
- 124,357 checks totaling $24 million passed out to farmers. In addition, coffee growers were granted a subsidy of $200 per hectare.[387]
- 17 rural stores run by the government agency CONASUPO.[388]

- $244 million provided to upgrade highways and build new ones.[389]
- Expanded educational programs such as providing for 30,700 additional elementary students and the creation of 100 secondary schools taught by television. Spanish literacy programs enrolled 74,000 adults while 50,000 were enrolled in literacy programs in indigenous languages. In addition, school breakfasts were being supplied to 143,250 children.[390]
- $12 million to provide infrastructure for low-cost medical service to be provided by the Mexican Social Security Institute.[391]
- 32 new centers were established to distribute subsidized tortillas and milk.[392]
- $1.35 million to benefit coffee, cacao, and corn producers in various parts of the state.[393]

The list of government-provided services and materials was seemingly endless. It also included new latrines, seeds for orchards, school supplies, fertilizer, insecticide, and cattle. Announced spending in Chiapas during 1994 totaled $298 million.[394]

Hernández Navarro commented on these government programs:

> Just as the EZLN has indicated, only part of the money spent reaches its intended beneficiaries, and some projects never get beyond the planning stage. Substantial payments for rent and damages have been used to "calm" cattlemen and estate owners. In addition, several "official" peasant organizations have been financed to guarantee their loyalty. Additional resources have been directed to productive projects which are chosen using discretionary criteria. This money continues to be allocated with virtually no input from the producers themselves.

Hernández Navarro also noted that the question of land ownership, the underlying problem, had been barely addressed.[395]

During the first half of 1994, business suffered as a result of the rebellion. An estimated 1,000 businesses closed, more than 3,000 people were laid off, and $30 million of debt went unpaid. Cattle ranchers suffered heavy losses.[396] By mid-October, Sergio Mota Marín, state secretary of economic development, estimated economic losses of $16 million due to the uprising, which also resulted in $1.47 billion lost to deferred investment. He also reported that tourism had declined by 70 percent.[397]

Commerce Secretary Jaime Serra Puche did promise a better future. He announced that 19 private investment projects were underway in Chiapas. These projects, totaling $1.47 billion, were projected to create 14,000 jobs in areas as diverse as farming and financial services. Serra Puche attributed the investments to the passage of NAFTA.[398]

The biggest single event of the summer was the National Democratic Convention (CND) which the EZLN had called for at the same time it rejected the proposed peace accords. The EZLN stated the goals for the convention were: 1) a transition to democracy in Mexico, 2) a national plan (*proyecto nacional*), 3) a transitional or caretaker government to manage the transition, and 4) preparation for a new constitution.[399] In the convocation for the convention, Marcos invited "those who struggle or want to struggle for democratic change. Those who do not want democratic change *are not invited*." Marcos also excluded those who want to rely exclusively on armed struggle to produce change, as well as those who do not feel that Mexico needs a transitional government, those who are not convinced Mexico needs a new constitution, and those who feel the PRI is not the main obstacle to democratic transition.[400]

Roughly 15,000 people applied for permission to attend the convention, but, due to logistical constraints, only 6,000 were accepted. Delegate slots were allocated by state, in rough proportion to population. The Federal District received 950 slots while states such as Quintana Roo and Hidalgo each received 100. In each state, groups representing trade unions, slum dwellers, Indians, peasants, and other constituencies selected delegates. Those attending were united only by their desire for major social change. They included intellectuals, feminists, students, guerrillas, peasants, labor activists, artisans, gays, writers, businessmen (a few), PRD members, Indians, the elderly, veterans of lost causes, artists, and veterans of the original Zapatista movement. PAN member Javier Livas Cantú even showed up "out of curiosity."[401] In addition, there were 711 journalists from 400 news organizations.[402]

On the first day of the convention, 6 August 1994, delegates met in San Cristóbal and divided into six groups. Each group attended a round table where a set of resolutions was passed.

The resolutions were:

Round table I: Transition to Democracy

- The Convention should initiate the transition toward a democratic society, which includes the elimination of the state party and of presidentialism.
- Voters in the 21 August elections should oppose the PRI.
- The assets of the PRI should be seized since they were obtained illegally.
- Members of civil society should actively participate in the 21 August elections as poll watchers and observers.

Round table II: The Peaceful Path to Democracy

- Voters in the 21 August elections should also oppose the PAN.
- The path to change should include elections, while keeping in mind that "the struggle for democracy, liberty, and justice in Mexico neither begins in nor ends with elections, which are only one aspect of the struggle for democracy."
- In case the elections are fraudulent, the Convention should organize peaceful resistance.

Round table III: Formulating a National Program

- The ideals of the Mexican Revolution have been betrayed.
- "Currently, a small group has taken over the government and uses its power to further its selfish interests. To keep themselves in power, its members have resorted to electoral fraud and co-optation and have generally neglected the responsibilities of leadership."
- The goal of the Convention is the establishment of a socially committed state which will implement the social goals enunciated in the initial communiqué of the EZLN.

Round table IV: The Characteristics of the Transitional Government

- The transitional government should be pluralistic and respect the popular will.

- The transitional government should put Carlos Salinas de Gortari, Patrocinio González Garrido, and other government officials on trial.

Round table V: The Constitutional Convention

- The current constitution has been so modified that the original social content of the 1917 document has been obliterated.
- A new constitution should be drafted which would include a provision for Indian rights, to be drafted by Indians, which would guarantee them legislative representation via special legislative seats.
- A new election law is needed to guarantee fair elections in the selection of delegates to the constitutional convention.[403]

Surprisingly, the state government not only tolerated the Convention but went out of its way to accommodate it. The government noted that conventioneers were merely exercising their constitutional right to assembly. Meeting sites were made available for the round tables held in San Cristóbal. In a successful effort to prevent violent confrontation between conventioneers and conservatives, the government prohibited the sale of alcoholic beverages while delegates were in San Cristóbal and provided police escorts as delegates left the city.

After one day in San Cristóbal, delegates piled onto 234 buses to travel 62 miles into EZLN-held territory. Some 23 hours later, after passing through Mexican-army and EZLN checkpoints and traversing muddy roads, they arrived at Aguascalientes, the site for the plenary session of the Convention. The Convention site was a newly constructed amphitheater near Guadalupe Tepeyac. The EZLN estimated that it had provided 235,200 hours of labor to prepare the Convention site.[404]

The site's name, Aguascalientes, was taken from the name of a city in north-central Mexico. In 1914, delegates of various revolutionary factions met there to plan Mexico's future and end the fratricidal struggle between revolutionary groups. Columnist Marco Rascón noted that naming the 1994 Convention site Aguascalientes focused on the positive aspects of the 1914 convention—social reform,

Conventioneers at Aguascalientes *Eduardo Vera*

transforming the political system, and the writing of new constitution.[405] Miguel Ángel Granados Chapa, however, noted that the real legacy of the Aguascalientes convention was a failure to come to agreement and a resumption of bloody strife among revolutionary factions.[406] Marcos addressed the failure of the original Aguascalientes convention: "Mexico is not the same country it was in 1914. It's much better, and that goes not only for civil society, but it should be noted, for the military as well."[407]

Delegates spent much more time traveling to and from Aguascalientes than they spent there. During the relatively short time they were in attendance, they ratified the resolutions of each of the round tables. Thus, the convention incorporated each set of resolutions as its position. Human-rights activist Rosario Ibarra de Piedra was chosen as president of the Convention. A 100-person steering committee was formed. Representatives from state delegations and prominent academics and political figures were chosen to serve on it. The committee was charged with organizing a second convention later in 1994. Proceedings were cut short when the nylon tarp covering the amphitheater blew down on convention members during a torrential rainstorm.

Even though Ibarra de Piedra was chosen president of the Convention, Marcos' presence dominated it. He addressed the assembled delegates: "We do not regret having risen in arms against the supreme government. We state once again that they left us no other course. ... We are ready to spill more blood, if that is the price we must pay for democratic change in Mexico."[408] Later, when asked what the weak point of the convention had been, he commented, "Well, the roof, obviously." He also reported another problem was getting delegates to leave, since many had wanted to join the EZLN.[409]

Given the diversity of the convention delegates, contradictions abounded. Most rejected traditional political parties but supported Cárdenas' candidacy. Solution: urging Mexicans to vote, and to oppose the PRI and the PAN. Convention delegates were highly solicitous of indigenous rights, but even there the path to follow was not clear. For example, Tzotzil activist Juana María Ruiz stated that change is needed in indigenous communities, too. She noted that Tzotzil women traditionally have not been able to own land or select marriage partners. Ruiz commented: "In the Constitution, it declares that indigenous customs must be respected. Well, we favor some traditions, but others must be changed."[410]

Women's participation in the CND showed the distance that women in Mexican society have advanced, as well as the challenges still facing them. They constituted roughly 40 percent of the delegates. Even that degree of participation was disappointing to some activists. They noted that the figure should have been higher, since women constitute more than 50 percent of the population, 56 percent of registered voters, and 80 percent of the popular urban movement. Critics also decried the selection of only 19 women for the 100-person CND steering committee. The female delegates did reflect the diversity of the CND itself, and included workers, peasants, Indians, artisans, gang members, journalists, artists, intellectuals, and writers.[411]

Delegates had hardly slogged their way back to San Cristóbal before another round of commentary began. Comments on the National Democratic Convention ranged from dismissing it as a leftist Woodstock to elevating it to the Mexican equivalent of the Continental Congress.

Columnist Humberto Musacchio declared the demands presented by the Convention were not unreasonable

> if we consider that during this six-year presidential term, one man, supported only by a legislative majority of dubious origin, drastically modified the Mexican Constitution so that it bears no resemblance to the document of 1917. Thus, it should not be surprising that the Zapatistas and other social groups demand a new constitution to serve the majority, and not the 24 billionaires listed in *Forbes* magazine.[412]

Miguel Ángel Granados Chapa noted that the accomplishments of the Convention included: 1) showing that the goals of the EZLN have wide backing nationwide, 2) making the EZLN a legitimate political force, and 3) showing the willingness of the EZLN to engage in a peaceful political process.[413]

Others did not know exactly what to make of the Convention. For example, authors Guido Camú Urzúa and Dauno Tótoro Taulis declared it was "not clear who will the lead the heterogeneous alliance emerging from the Convention, whether they will be pro-democracy members of the PRI, the EZLN, the PRD, Marcos, Camacho Solís, or Cuauhtémoc Cárdenas."[414]

Critics also abounded. Columnist Marcario Schettino declared that the National Democratic Convention was neither national nor democratic.[415] Similarly, José Luis Soberanes Fernández noted that roughly 90 million Mexicans had nothing to do with repudiating the existing constitution, as the Convention demanded.[416] Convention organizers screened out and denied access to journalists from a long list of media organizations. This put into question their commitment to freedom of expression. Such a commitment is especially important if organizers hope to extend their influence from largely rural Chiapas to the rest of mostly urban Mexico.[417]

Marcos commented that the Convention began the building of a grass-roots, nationwide network. He charged the delegates: "You have to take these resolutions to the barrios, to the ejidos, to the indigenous communities. Then we can indeed speak of being on the road to democracy."[418] Just as it was impossible to evaluate the impact of the 1974 indigenous conference in San Cristóbal until decades later, time must pass before it will be clear if the Convention sowed the seeds for change or was just a fleeting event.

Attention almost immediately shifted from the Convention to the elections of 21 August. These elections chose Mexico's next president, the entire Mexican Congress, and the next governor of Chiapas. Some 200 grass-roots organizations in Chiapas backed Amado Avendaño, the PRD gubernatorial candidate. Avendaño is one of the few Chiapan lawyers willing to defend Indians and their causes. One of his clients was Joel Padrón, the jailed priest. In addition, along with his wife Concepción Villafuerte Blanco, he edited *Tiempo*, a small newspaper in San Cristóbal which has been the sole source of much news screened out by the dominant, conservative press.

On 25 July 1994, the car Avendaño was riding in was hit head-on by a tractor-trailer truck. Three members of Avendaño's campaign staff were killed, and he was critically injured. Avendaño's wife claimed the crash was a criminal act, noting that the truck had no license plates and no cargo, and that the driver had swerved into the path of the Avendaño's campaign vehicle. The driver of the truck fled after the crash.[419] Gov. López Moreno declared the crash an "accident." Just as with the Colosio murder, the circumstances surrounding the collision remain in doubt and many see it as an attempt to murder Avendaño.

Avendaño was flown to a Mexico City hospital in critical condition. While he was in the hospital, teams of supporters kept his campaign going, visiting towns and holding rallies at which videos of his speeches were shown.

Avendaño's condition improved, permitting him to return to Chiapas after 16 days. There he declared, "We are faced with a government apparatus which is dying and which clings to power and extends its tentacles to block the way of those who dare to challenge it."[420] Avendaño promised that, if elected, he would head a transitional government which would write a new state constitution and then call truly democratic elections. At the closing rally of his campaign, his daughter Elía read a statement on behalf of the still convalescing candidate. The statement declared: "I'm not here of my own free will. I'm here because the Supreme Creator rescued me from the jaws of death to fulfill a destiny which has not yet been revealed to me."[421]

Avendaño's main opponent was Eduardo Robledo, who served as state secretary of education under Absalón Castellanos. He was a member of a group of Castellanos' young protégés called the "diaper gang."[422] At the time of his nomination as PRI gubernatorial candidate, Robledo was serving as senator. Political scientist Garrido noted that the PRI candidate was selected by *dedazo*—that is, presidential designation—and that his appointment as candidate indicates that the PRI was continuing its undemocratic procedures as if nothing had happened in the state during the previous months.[423] Both his undemocratic selection and his association with Castellanos give Robledo high negative ratings in Chiapas.

When he was sworn in as the PRI candidate, Robledo struck a conciliatory note. He stated, "I am aware of what it means to be a candidate for governor of the state of Chiapas at this time. I will stress the importance of forgetting grievances, of healing wounds, of re-establishing harmony, of promoting peace and unity."[424] Strikingly absent from his declarations was any pledge to implement significant social change and thus alleviate the root causes of the rebellion.

Robledo ran a well-financed campaign. He even paid for a newspaper story in a Mexico City paper which reported that he was "worried" that the EZLN was more concerned with national issues such as democracy than it was with the well-being of Indians in Chiapas.[425]

To help sway potential voters, the PRI channeled money to certain individuals within the CEOIC who supported Robledo. These individuals were declared to constitute the "legitimate" CEOIC. Those opposed to Robledo were branded as "PRD members," even though many of them did not want to either participate in electoral politics or have anything to do with the PRD.[426]

After the election, Robledo was declared governor-elect with 51.1 percent of the vote, compared to Avendaño's 34.1 percent and the PAN candidate's 9.4 percent.[427] The election returns were accompanied by a flood of protests concerning the conduct of the elections. Avendaño declared that, in many cases, tally sheets were switched before being delivered to the state election commission and that totals on others had been altered.[428]

The Civic Alliance, a non-partisan election-monitoring group, noted that irregularities in Chiapas were far above the national average. They included a lack of voting secrecy at 67.82 percent of polling places, coercion at 44.54 percent, flying squads voting repeatedly at 11.33 percent, and ballot stuffing at 8.95 percent.[429]

Journalist John Ross reported that ballots were in oversupply in areas likely to favor the PRI. However, if an area was perceived as hostile to the PRI, there were often ballot shortages. Thus, for example, only 506 ballots arrived at ejido Morelia, even though the ejido and the 12 surrounding communities which voted there required 1,500 ballots.[430]

The PRD charged that there were irregularities at 90 percent of the polling places. At polling station 1031 in Pijijiapan, the 604 registered voters reportedly cast 1,053 votes for the PRI.[431] Other sources noted widespread vote buying.[432] Referring to the many U.S. election observers, Marcos commented that "only the gringos" could believe the officially reported returns.[433]

The most positive election reports emerged from the area dominated by the EZLN, where 67 polling places were established. There, elderly Indians reported that they had a chance to vote for the first time in their life. Previously, huge PRI majorities were simply announced. Not surprisingly, the PRI only received 23.43 percent of the vote in EZLN-controlled areas.[434]

The official results of the August election did provide a quantifiable indicator of the change which swept Chiapas. The PRD in the state received 724 percent more votes than Cuauhtémoc Cárdenas had received in the state in 1988. The PRI vote, in contrast, declined by 17 percent between 1988 and 1994.[435]

At the end of August, Marcos wrote to the officially designated governor-elect, commenting, "Speaking as one transgressor to another, I must confess that I feel you outdid your predecessor in the last election." Marcos promised that if Robledo would resign, Marcos would write the court which would try Robledo for electoral fraud and he would plead for mercy. Marcos also said he would intercede on Robledo's behalf when he was tried by Zapatista courts for complicity in crimes committed by former governors Castellanos Domínguez and González Garrido.[436]

The disputed elections increased tension in the state. In early September, peasants occupied nine coffee, cattle, and banana estates, with the declared purpose of protesting the spurious elections and "to recuperate lands which historically have belonged to us and which are in the hands of caciques and landlords."[437] Thousands of others protested the elections by blocking highways and seizing radio stations to broadcast Avendaño's declarations.[438]

Neither the convention nor the elections served to return Chiapas to normalcy. Negotiations remained stalled. On 23 June, Jorge

Madrazo, who was serving as director of the National Commission for Human Rights, was appointed as peace negotiator to replace Camacho Solís. On 1 July, he sent the EZLN a message "inviting it to jointly explore the form and terms for resuming the route to peace."[439] Three months later, talks had still not resumed. Madrazo publicly inquired why the EZLN did not want dialogue and reaffirmed that "the government of the republic is ready to negotiate in order to reach a peace with justice and dignity in Chiapas."[440]

Madrazo, however, put negotiations into question. He made the following comment about democracy—the stumbling block in the first round: "The demand for democracy is something which I cannot resolve. It has to be resolved at the ballot box."[441] Convention President Ibarra relayed a message from Marcos when she spoke at an Independence Day rally at the National University. She reported that, before talks could begin, federal troops must be removed from Chiapas and Avendaño must be allowed to take office as governor.[442]

As the scheduled December inaugurations of Ernesto Zedillo as president and Eduardo Robledo as governor approached, the likelihood of renewed peace talks receded. In an 8 October communiqué, the EZLN declared that it was rejecting peace talks and that the rebels had set up anti-aircraft batteries and mined roads into their territory.[443]

In an interview later in the month, Marcos stated that this behavior was in response to government actions. He charged that the day after the 21 August elections, government troops had begun threatening maneuvers. He also reported repeated overflights by government military aircraft in an apparent attempt to draw fire from rebels and thus provoke renewed combat.[444]

There was little in Marcos' message that could be seen as conciliatory. He belittled newly appointed peace negotiator Jorge Madrazo, claiming that he had only been appointed to pull the wool over people's eyes. Marcos also declared that, if fighting broke out again, the conflict would not be confined to Chiapas. He stated, "We are not lying when we say our army is throughout the country." Furthermore, Marcos claimed that other guerrilla groups in Guerrero, Michoacán, Oaxaca, Puebla, Hidalgo, Tabasco, and Veracruz could bolster the EZLN in case of renewed hostilities.[445]

Marcos also saw the PRI and the lame-duck Salinas administration as being so divided that it would be useless to negotiate with them. On referring to PRI Secretary General José Francisco Ruiz Massieu, who was assassinated on 28 September in what is generally considered to be a PRI faction fight, Marcos said, "We don't know with whom we are going to speak, whether it is with the assassins of Ruiz Massieu or with the faction of the assassinated."[446]

Hernández Navarro commented on the EZLN's reluctance to plunge into negotiations again. He noted that, during the first round of negotiations, the Salinas administration had scored three big public-relations victories. They were: 1) the removal from consideration of Salinas' resignation, 2) keeping the conflict from interfering with the 21 August election, and 3) giving Salinas the image of being a negotiator. Hernández Navarro also noted that the 8 October communiqué reflected the mixed messages received by the EZLN from the government. On the one hand, the government stated that it wanted negotiations. Yet, on the other hand, it repressed peasants as power ebbed at the end of the presidential term. In addition, as the assassination of Ruiz Massieu showed, there was internal strife inside the PRI, making it difficult to negotiate with.[447]

Political scientist Garrido saw other reasons for not resuming dialogue, which included: 1) the government's feeling that Indian leaders could be bought off as in the past, 2) the government's unwillingness to accept social change to obtain peace, and 3) the failure to realize that Chiapans want land, liberty, their own culture, and control of forests and rivers, not a job at McDonald's—the best thing Salinas' development model offers them.[448]

The government continued to call for peace and resumed negotiations. In response to the 8 October EZLN communiqué, Salinas stated that he still wanted a peaceful, negotiated settlement to the conflict.[449] On 18 October, Madrazo offered to create a fact-finding commission to pave the way for a new round of peace talks. He also offered to station human-rights monitors at army road blocks.[450] On 1 November, in his last state-of-the-nation address, Salinas declared, "Here, before the representatives of the nation, I am renewing my call for dialogue to convert conflict into solutions, into civil respect, and into progress."[451] The EZLN either ignored or rejected each of these overtures.

During the fall of 1994, the Chiapas issue largely faded from the national and international press. However, normalcy had yet to return to Chiapas. In addition to the question of resuming negotiations, the upcoming gubernatorial inauguration kept the state on tenterhooks. In October, Marcos linked the inauguration of Robledo to renewed violence, noting, "If Robledo is imposed as governor, there is going to be war here." He added, "'Here' means Mexico, not just Chiapas."[452] He also saw Chiapas as becoming ungovernable, noting: "Things will blow up because of the problems created by imposing Robledo. He faces not only an armed movement, but an uncontrollable, peaceful civilian movement."[453]

While awaiting his scheduled inauguration, Robledo adopted a conciliatory position similar to that of the Salinas administration. He commented, "In Chiapas, society is in a precarious position, as a result of a long history of offenses, poverty, neglect, and abuse."[454] Robledo did vow to take office as scheduled in December, noting: "I am the first one to ask that anyone who charges fraud prove it. Those who have evidence of fraud and do not present it are engaging in a cover-up. We cannot disregard the effort of the people of Chiapas and of all the political parties."[455]

While leaders of both sides waged their war of words, the rank and file mobilized. On 3 October, protesters took over city halls in Pantelhó, Soyaló, Calahuitán, and Villa Corzo. Their common demand was the ouster of mayors and more farm support from the government program Procampo.[456] In mid-October, more than 300 protesters armed with clubs and machetes took over the city hall in Simojovel and freed four prisoners from the adjacent jail. They demanded the ouster of the mayor for taking public funds. This takeover raised to three the number of city halls held by indigenous dissidents demanding the ouster of mayors.[457] In addition, several highways were blocked by protesters who would demand "voluntary" payments of from $6 to $15 to allow vehicles to pass.[458]

On Columbus Day, more than 25,000 indigenous people attended a pro-Avendaño rally in San Cristóbal. Some walked for days to reach the rally, barefoot or in sandals. Many were indigenous women wearing brightly colored clothing and ribbons wrapped into their braids, with unique patterns indicating their village of origin. When they arrived in San Cristóbal, they once again adorned the city with revolutionary graffiti proclaiming "Viva EZLN, Viva Marcos," "Death to capitalist assassins," and "We have taken San Cristóbal *again*." Another slogan, referring to the light-skinned elite by the term they fancy—the "authentic" residents—demanded, "Authentics, go back

Avendaño rally in San Cristóbal *Eduardo Vera*

to Spain!" Since they were unwilling to deal with the unwelcome arrivals, most shopkeepers simply closed for the day.

At the rally, a message from Marcos was read, rejecting "a governor who is not ours" and declaring, "We prefer to die rather than living with the shame of having a tyrant dictating our actions and our words." A CEOIC communiqué was also read which declared nine areas of the state to be multi-ethnic regions and the towns in them to be autonomous. The decree noted, "Only our governor-elect, Amado Avendaño, and his representatives will be recognized as our authorities." Finally, the CEOIC declared that neither taxes nor water and electric bills would be paid to the "usurper government."[459]

While they were less numerous than the Avendaño supporters, cattlemen were equally vociferous in denouncing their loss of land. Having failed to goad the state government into assisting them recoup the 2,157 estates they claimed were occupied, landowners organized an auto caravan to Mexico City to press their case at the national level. They rejected an appeal from Gov. López Moreno to delay the caravan, noting: "We're tired of hearing the same thing. They're always asking for more time. We've waited long enough. Ten months have passed since the conflict broke out. For four of these months, we were sitting in front of the state capital. They never did what they agreed to."[460]

After the caravan arrived in Mexico City, 117 of its members began a hunger strike along the Paseo de la Reforma, a major thoroughfare. Unlike indigenous protesters, the Chiapas cattlemen had their own TVs and cellular phones.

As Robledo's scheduled inauguration approached, each side had backed itself into a corner, making it difficult to attempt some face-saving gesture such as the appointment of a commission to study the problem. The PRI steadfastly declared that it would inaugurate the legally elected candidate as scheduled. Given the mood of the opposition, it was unlikely that the tactic repeatedly used by the Salinas administration—the appointment of a stand-in for the person initially declared winner—would be accepted by the EZLN and its allies. Repression—another tactic resorted to under the Salinas administration—would risk alienating those supporters, many of whose support was at best tepid, who voted for Zedillo. It would also scare off foreign investors and risk bogging the government down in a prolonged guerrilla war in difficult terrain.

The opposition stated that its strategy, rather than simply waiting for Robledo's inauguration, was to force President Salinas to step in and declare Avendaño governor-elect before inauguration day. Thus, Robledo opponents began taking city halls, land, and radio stations, blocking highways, and closing government services such as clinics and schools well before the scheduled inauguration. CEOIC leader Jorge Arturo Luna described these actions as being designed to show that "it is impossible to govern by force and that it is no longer possible to impose state authorities by electoral fraud."[461]

The second plenary session of the National Democratic Convention was held in Tuxtla Gutiérrez during the first weekend of November. The main themes on the agenda were a response to the August elections, peace in Chiapas, and the CND's own structure. The 2,500 delegates declared their support for "honest dialogue between the federal government and the EZLN which would guarantee a dignified, just peace and the peaceful transition to democracy." The CND also called for demonstrations and national work stoppages on 1 December and 8 December, the scheduled dates of Zedillo's and

Government troops in Altamirano — *Paulina Hermosillo*

Robledo's inaugurations, respectively. Finally, the CND formed a National Council of Representatives, composed of three representatives from each state, as well as additional members representing peasants, the indigenous, workers, artists, intellectuals, human-rights workers, sociologists, students, and women.[462]

The CND successfully dealt with radicals within its ranks, considered its association with the EZLN, and laid the groundwork for ties with other progressive groups. However, one thing was clear—the second plenary session captured far less media attention than had the first. If the number of column inches of press coverage correlates to the CND's goal of promulgating a new constitution, that goal seems further away.

The prolonged military standoff continued. Rebels claimed that their territory was surrounded by 50,000 troops, while the army claimed there were only 20,000.[463] Journalist Nancy Nusser noted: "The Zapatistas sit, all but militarily powerless, in an enclave, surrounded by government troops. Meanwhile, the government is working to wipe out the discontent that fueled the movement by putting jobless peasants to work."[464] Historian García de León noted that, in the absence of combat, the army

> acts increasingly like an army of occupation with all that implies. Dispirited, bored, far from their families, they channel their frustration toward the defenseless peasants who must cross their military checkpoints. The rape of two young Tzeltal women at the Altamirano checkpoint—and the soldiers seeing Zapatistas in every peasant that dares look them in the eye—contributes to this increasing tension.[465]

The significance of Zedillo's election is unclear. When campaigning in Tuxtla on 5 May, Zedillo stated: "I am proposing major social reform because my strongest commitment is to those who have the least. This social reform will signify more and better housing, more dignified services, and more schools and hospitals of higher quality, and more opportunity for everyone." Zedillo promised: "I am committed to the small business owners of Chiapas, because they generate the jobs that you are demanding and are a source of income for everyone. We are going to facilitate small businessmen's access to credit."[466]

Marcos, however, saw Zedillo in a different light. He commented: "Luis Donaldo Colosio had a flexible attitude with respect to this problem. However, I see Zedillo as very intolerant, very close-minded."[467]

Chapter 12: Conclusion

> What happened in Chiapas is a great lesson for the country. Modernization cannot ignore the cultural and historic roots of Mexico. Economic change should include responses to the necessities of social groups which have remained on the sidelines of development.
>
> — Manuel Camacho Solís[468]

Even before the first round of negotiations began, sociologist Rodolfo Stavenhagen commented that possible results of the Chiapas uprising included: 1) a mutually agreed upon, negotiated settlement; 2) prolonged talks, repression, and a slow crumbling of the movement; 3) fighting extending into other parts of Mexico; or 4) prolonged war as has gone on for decades in places such as the Sudan, the Philippines, and Guatemala.[469] The possibility of a military solution might seem attractive to hard-liners. However, as Carlos Montemayor notes: "The EZLN could become a complex network of guerrilla commands which would be impossible to detect and neutralize in the short run. A purely military response would take years. The national and international cost of the repression would be incalculable."[470] Marcos has vowed to attack Chiapas' abundant energy-production facilities if the government launches a military offensive.[471]

Although the immediate problems afflicting Chiapas are social and economic, there is a consensus that a long-term solution to these problems will necessitate removing the entrenched political group which protects the status quo.[472]

David Asman of the *Wall Street Journal* feels that the need to woo investors will lead to political concessions in Chiapas. He noted:

> What is clear is that Mexico's economic opening can no longer be sustained if guarantees of political openness and unconditional respect for the political will of Mexicans are not forthcoming. Without such guarantees, political stability can no longer be assured. And without political stability, investment in Mexico cannot be secured.[473]

Simply identifying Chiapas' political clique as an impediment to investment does not guarantee its removal. In fact, as political scientist Arnaldo Córdova commented: "The armed rebellion dispersed the elite caste in the region like a hurricane. The leaders of the EZLN should take note that the elite has gathered itself again and is ready to fight for its privileges, which could make peace negotiations fail."[474]

Since Chiapas is heavily agricultural, addressing economic problems involves deciding how to organize agriculture. Historian John Womack, Jr., the biographer of Zapata, noted that putting more people on the land is not the way out of poverty. Mexico already has 25 percent of its population in agriculture, while industrialized countries only have 4 to 5 percent. Womack thus advocates taking people out of agriculture, not putting them in, as a cure for poverty.[475]

Ivan Restrepo warns of the danger of considering tropical areas, such as Chiapas, as breadbaskets. He notes that agricultural development projects already attempted in Chiapas and other tropical states have been complete failures. The only ones to have benefited have been corrupt officials who got rich. The projects themselves only created new social, economic, and cultural problems.[476] Land availability also limits the degree to which agriculture can resolve Chiapas' problems. In 1910, there were 16.8 hectares per capita. By 1990, this figure had declined to 2.3 hectares.[477]

Others, such as anthropologist Neil Harvey, are more optimistic concerning agriculture. He feels that agricultural solutions to rural poverty are feasible if a value is placed on factors such as native culture as well as market profitability. Harvey comments that, for this to happen, public investment in infrastructure, marketing, technical assistance, and pricing mechanisms would be needed. He notes that such measures are "the type of policies that every advanced industrialized country implemented to create modern and viable agricultural sectors." A key to any such viability would be "the

Near Guadalupe Tepeyac *Paulina Hermosillo*

dissolution of political controls, which in rural Mexico have traditionally been associated with *caciquismo.*"[478]

Harvey cites as a positive example of modernization the growing of organic coffee by the *Unión de Ejidos de la Selva.* This group processes the coffee it grows and markets it abroad. The entire operation is under the producers' control, and they retain all of the profits. Another example is the Aztec Harvest Company, which is collectively owned by small farmers in four Mexican states. It sells coffee to U.S. specialty shops and Ben & Jerry's ice cream.[479] As Harvey notes, "Indians want to participate in modernizing society, but as independent actors, not as cheap labor, and in Chiapas they are the cheapest cheap labor there is."[480]

Marcos has commented on the necessity of investment in Chiapas:

> The problem of the land is one of productivity, not of extension or tenancy. Not even the expropriation of large estates will solve the problem because there is not enough land in the state. The problem of the land is productivity. It will be necessary not only to subdivide estates and regularize land titles, but to make massive investment in infrastructure, which will increase yield per hectare. In the Lacandón jungle, the average yield is half a ton of corn per hectare, while in the rest of the country is it eight tons per hectare.[481]

Investment needs are overwhelming. A publication of Solidarity noted: "In this zone, there are few roads, and almost all are bad. Construction is very expensive, and maintenance costs even more."[482] The scattered settlement pattern adds to costs. In the municipalities of Ocosingo, Altamirano, Las Margaritas, and Palenque, there are 1,209 communities of three or more houses, and an additional 9,137 locations with one or two houses. Almost 250,000 people in these municipalities reside outside the municipal seats.[483] These isolated settlements are scattered over an area larger than some Central American or European nations.[484] Poor planning and insufficient support of colonization projects at their inception have increased the cost of addressing current problems.[485]

Given pressing needs throughout Mexico, the question arises of just how much should be invested in the EZLN-controlled area of Chiapas. In some areas, the land is so poor that seven hectares is needed to support one cow. As Armando Bartra commented: "There are a lot of Chiapans, and nature in the state is exuberant but intractable. Good soils are scarce. The rain forest will not support a great population density, and it must be treated with care." Bartra also noted, "Given the reality of negative growth in the national per capita product, and profound agricultural deficiencies, setting the Chiapan economy on an environmentally sound path of social justice is cyclopean."[486]

Many fear long-term environmental concerns in Chiapas will be abandoned in an attempt to satisfy peasant land hunger. Ignacio March, a researcher at the Southeastern Ecology Research Center, comments: "We are extremely concerned that among the solutions proposed will be subdividing the jungle. There is no other federal land in the state that can be distributed. The risk is very high."[487]

Sacrificing the jungle would be politically expedient for both the government and the EZLN. Given pressing survival needs, such abstract concepts as ecology are not priorities among many Lancandón residents. One Zapatista woman commented on ecologists: "All they tell us is not to cut the trees, not to burn the land—but how can we not do so when we have to eat?"[488] Rather than accepting such "easy" solutions as carving up the jungle, the EZLN advocates dividing up large estates to supply land for the landless.[489]

Marcos has observed that the implementation of the North American Free Trade Agreement (NAFTA) presents a problem for Chiapas: "NAFTA is a death sentence because it leads to competition based on your level of skill, and what skill level can illiterate people have? And look at this land. How can we compete with farms in California and Canada?"[490]

The issue of maintaining Indian cultures in the midst of a rapidly changing and increasingly integrated world also presents complex problems. As Womack notes:

> The issue is how to preserve Indian institutions, values, and ways of life in the midst of rapid changes, and even Indians agree that this is a very difficult question. The problem is that they say they want schools, hospitals, roads, good jobs. How can you have that and preserve institutions at the same time? It seems to me a bit like the situation in Algeria, where fundamentalist Islamic groups want both modernity and a preservation of their traditions.[491]

Anthropologist Andrés Medina notes that social and economic changes undergone by Indian communities in the past 50 years have made the notion of autonomy much harder to apply. He comments,

San Mateo Zapotal, Las Margaritas *Duncan Earle*

"The Indian population is no longer composed exclusively of peasants working in a cornfield and maintaining ancient wisdom. Nor are they all wrapped in a cosmic view based in ancient Mesoamerica. They no longer exclusively speak an Indian language in some distant jungle, mountain, or farming community." Rather, the Indian population has diversified into cattle raising and commercial agriculture. Some work as wage laborers, while others have migrated to cities, including those in the United States. Yet, they still form a vital part of Indian communities and retain that identity.[492]

Changes in Indian life are pronounced in eastern Chiapas, the heartland of the EZLN. There, Tzeltals and Tzotzils from highland Chiapas have been joined by non-Indians from other Mexican states. They have rapidly evolved, shedding their ethnic identities for a more generic peasant identity. This identity is reflected in new ways of peasant organizing, community mobilization, and religious expression, as reflected in the many Protestant groups in the area.[493]

Settlement of the conflict will require clarity on basic issues involving Indians. The demand for Indian autonomy must be weighed against the need for change in Indian communities, as Tzotzil activist Juana María Ruiz commented. Embracing the status quo would leave many caciques in power, much as FDR's Good Neighbor policy left in power many Latin American dictators previously installed by U.S. Marines.

Another issue to be clarified is whether issues are more economic or ethnic—that is, whether the struggle is basically one of class or ethnicity. In eastern Chiapas, where virtually all Indians are poor, this issue is easy to ignore. However, in Indian towns such as Oxchuc, and even more so in Zinacantán, there is sharp economic stratification among those who are Indian.[494]

Regardless of whether the rebels and the government can come to a formal agreement, one undeniable effect of the 1994 New Year's rebellion was bringing substantial aid to Chiapas. Keeping the Zapatistas together as a viable force may prove more difficult than obtaining aid. Judiciously combining tangible rewards, the co-opting of individuals, and selective repression is something the government has done successfully for decades. The rebels will be hard put to survive the financial embrace of the state.

Notes

CHAPTER 1

[1] *El Financiero International* (14 Feb. 1994, p. 6).

[2] The *Washington Post* (7 Jan. 1994, p. A12).

[3] The *Wall Street Journal* (21 Jan. 1994, p. A15).

[4] De Vos (1992: 99).

[5] Gosner (1992) described the rebellion in detail. The Florescano quotation is from *La Jornada* (10 Jan. 1994, p. 18).

[6] *Reforma* (23 Jan. 1994, p. 7A).

[7] García de León (1985: I, 91).

[8] Benjamin (1989: 20) & *Proceso* (10 Jan. 1994, p. 48).

[9] *Proceso* (7 March 1994, p. 12). In a few areas, such as the municipality of Zinacantán, Indians have diversified economically into activities such as trading, construction work, trucking, and government employment (Cancian & Brown 1994). Such occurrences, however, remain an exception.

[10] *La Jornada del Campo* (25 Jan. 1993, p. 2).

[11] *Reforma* (16 Jan. 1994, p. 7A).

[12] *Proceso* (24 Jan. 1994, p. 30).

[13] *Perfil de la Jornada* (19 Jan. 1994, p. iii).

[14] Benjamin (1989: 89).

[15] Benjamin (1989: 92).

[16] García de León (1985: II, 50).

[17] Bartra (1994: 30) & Nigh (1994: 9).

[18] Quoted in Del Muro (1994: 22).

[19] Benjamin (1989: 179) & Harvey (1994b: 21).

[20] Guillermoprieto (1994: 52).

[21] García de León (1985: II, 225-26).

[22] Benjamin (1989: 197-208), Collier (1994: 14), García de León (1985: II, 199-218), and Knight (1994: 6) comment on Chiapas during the Cárdenas administration.

[23] Harvey (1994b: 28).

[24] *La Jornada del Campo* (25 Jan. 1994, p. 2).

[25] *Proceso* (7 Feb. 1994, p. 17).

[26] *Excélsior* (7 March 1994, p. 4A).

[27] Burbach (1994: 120).

[28] The *Los Angeles Times* (5 Jan. 1994, p. A11).

[29] Population figures are from *VI Censo de Población 1940*, Vol. 3, p. 13 & *XI Censo de Población y Vivienda 1990*, Vol. 7, Tomo 1, p. 4.

[30] *Proceso* (10 January 1994, p. 46).

[31] Casas & Castellanos (1994: 16).

[32] *Doblejornada* (7 March 1994, p. 13). Another synopsis of the daily life of indigenous women, by EZLN Capitan Maribel, appeared in the *Austin Chronicle* (4 Nov. 1994, p. 24).

[33] *La Jornada del Campo* (22 Feb. 1994, p. 9).

[34] Hernández Navarro (1994a: 45).

[35] Hernández Castillo (1992: 97).

[36] Rodríquez (1987: 314).

[37] *La Jornada del Campo* (25 Jan. 1994, p. 3).

[38] *Proceso* (24 Jan. 1994, p. 21).

[39] The *New York Times* (9 Jan. 1994, Sec. 4, p. 6) published the space photo.

[40] Harvey (1994b: 30).

[41] *La Jornada del Campo* (25 Jan. 1994, p. 3).

[42] Berberán *et al.* (1988: 124).

[43] *Proceso* (10 Jan. 1994, p. 39).

[44] *Macrópolis* (28 Feb. 1994, p. 10).

[45] The *Economist* (22 Jan. 1994, p. 21).

[46] *Reforma* (3 Aug. 1994, p. 10A).

[47] *La Jornada del Campo* (25 Jan. 1994, p. 2), *Fem* (April 1994, p. 19) & the *Wall Street Journal* (11 Feb. 1994, p. A13).

[48] The *San Francisco Chronicle* (21 Jan. 1994, A1), Gossen (1994), and Minnesota Advocates for Human Rights (1992: 52-55) discuss expulsions.

[49] *La Jornada* (24 Feb. 1994, p. 10).

[50] Benjamin (1989: xiv-xv).

[51] Harvey (1994b: 34).

[52] Minnesota Advocates for Human Rights (1992: 40-48).

[53] The *Christian Science Monitor* (3 March 1994, p. 7).

[54] Minnesota Advocates for Human Rights (1992: 25—emphasis in original).

[55] Gijsbers (1994: 24).

[56] Minnesota Advocates for Human Rights (1992: 26).

[57] Hernández Navarro (1994a: 45).

[58] Harvey (1994b: 33).

[59] Reding (1994: 13-14).

[60] *Proceso* (31 Jan. 1994, p. 41).

[61] *Proceso* (11 Jan. 1993, p. 7).

[62] Russell (1994: 154).

[63] *Proceso* (14 Feb. 1994, p. 29).

[64] *Proceso* (14 Feb. 1994, p. 15).

[65] *Proceso* (10 Jan. 1994, p. 35) quoted the report. *Horizontes,* the magazine of the Fray Bartolomé de las Casas Human Rights Center, has abundant information on human rights in Chiapas. Amnesty International (1986) and Minnesota Advocates for Human Rights (1992) considered human rights in Chiapas. Russell (1994: 140-59) discussed human rights in Mexico.

[66] The *Wall Street Journal* (11 Feb. 1994, p. A15).

[67] Piñeyro (1994: 6) & Rodríguez (1987: 302).

[68] Benjamin (1989: 77).

[69] Morris (1994: 16) & Toledo (1994: 9).

[70] *El Financiero International* (24 Jan. 1994, p. 13).

[71] Reding (1994: 16).

[72] Harvey (1994b: 9).

[73] Benjamin (1989: 230), *El Financiero* (15 March 1994, p. 61), *El Financiero International* (24 Jan. 1994, p. 13) & *La Jornada del Campo* (22 Feb. 1994, p. 10).

[74] Collier (1994: 16).

[75] Baitenmann (1994: 3).

[76] Harvey (1994b: 9-10), Bailón (1994: 22) & *La Jornada* (24 Jan. 1994, p. 6).

[77] Del Muro (1994: 21).
[78] Hernández Navarro (1994c: 4).
[79] *El Financiero International* (27 June 1994, p. 16).
[80] Harvey (1994b: 12).
[81] Hernández Navarro (1994a: 50).
[82] *Proceso* (14 Feb. 1994, p. 32).
[83] Harvey (1994b: 6).
[84] Rodríguez (1987: 304).
[85] *El Financiero* (5 Jan. 1994, p. 27).
[86] *Proceso* (24 Jan. 1994, p. 31).
[87] *La Jornada del Campo* (22 Feb. 1994, p. 8).
[88] *Excélsior* (23 Jan. 1994, p. 18A).
[89] The *Economist* (22 Jan. 1994, p. 13).
[90] Benjamin (1989: 50).
[91] *El Financiero International* (10 Jan. 1994, p. 6).
[92] *Forbes* (23 July 1990, p. 121 & 18 July 1994, pp. 194-95).
[93] *La Jornada del Campo* (22 Feb. 1994, p. 8).
[94] *Proceso* (15 May 1989, p. 12) quoted Pesqueira.
[95] *Gaceta de Solidaridad* (15 Jan. 1994, p. 4).
[96] *El Financiero* (5 Jan. 1994, p. 27).
[97] *Excélsior* (16 Jan. 1994, p. 10A).
[98] *La Jornada del Campo* (22 Feb. 1994, p. 13).
[99] *Macrópolis* (7 March 1994, p. 15).
[100] Conger (1994: 118), *El Financiero* (14 March 1994, p. 61), *El Financiero International* (24 Jan. 1994, p. 15) & *Proceso* (17 Jan. 1994, p. 70).
[101] Díaz-Polanco (1994: 19).
[102] Moguel (1994: 17).
[103] *La Jornada* (14 March 1994, p. 9).
[104] Urbina Nandayapa (1994: 60).

CHAPTER 2

[105] *All Things Considered* (Jan. 2, 1994 [transcript], pp. 1-2).
[106] *El Financiero* (16 March 1994, p. 64).
[107] Urbina Nandayapa (1994: 58).
[108] *El Financiero* (3 Jan. 1994, p. 44) & Urbina Nandayapa (1994: 60).
[109] *Proceso* (10 Jan. 1994, p. 10).
[110] Romero Jacobo (1994a: 67).
[111] *El Financiero* (16 March 1994, p. 64) noted the approach from Palenque. Human Rights Watch/Americas (1994: 16), *La Jornada* (3 Jan. 1994, p. 5), and Ross (1994: 89-94) also commented on Ocosingo. In a somewhat different reconstruction of events, Ross reported on EZLN forces being surprised by government troops coming from Palenque, without mentioning their boarding trucks and returning. In any event, the disastrous defense of the market ensued. Marcos later spoke of the "errors of Ocosingo" (*El Financiero,* 2 March 1994, p. 48). The rebel view of the battle was presented in *¡Ya Basta!* (June 1994, pp. 27-32).
[112] *Reforma* (5 Jan. 1994, p. 5A).
[113] *Proceso* (10 Jan. 1994, p. 13).

[114] Romero Jacobo (1994a: 67) & Collier (1994: 17-18).

[115] *El Financiero* (9 Jan. 1994, p. 1).

[116] *La Jornada* (7 Feb. 1994, p. 9).

[117] *La Jornada* (11 June 1994, p. 6). The CNDH did not specifically enumerate EZLN combatants killed. Presumably they fall in the "unidentified" category.

[118] *La Jornada* (23 Feb. 1994, p. 10).

[119] *Proceso* (7 Feb. 1994, p. 7).

[120] The *Economist* (8 Jan. 1994, p. 41), Human Rights Watch/Americas (1994: 10) & Ross (1994: 104).

[121] *Reforma* (18 Jan. 1994, p. 5A) quoted the resident. Human Rights Watch/ Americas (1994: 21-22) and Ross (1994: 113-19) reported on Ejido Morelia.

[122] Amnesty International (1994) summarized the findings. *Proceso* (14 Feb. 1994, p. 14) quoted Tidball. *Justicia y Paz* (Jan.-March 1994, pp. 68-71, 78-80) reported other abuses by the army. Other descriptions of human-rights abuses include Comisión Mexicana de Defensa y Promoción de los Derechos Humanos *et al.* (1994), Méndez Asenio & Cano Gimeno (1994: 194-99), Ross (1994: 122-33), Tovar Nieves (1994), and a series entitled *Special Bulletin: Chiapas in Conflict* published from January to March of 1994 by the Academia Mexicana de Derechos Humanos.

[123] Human Rights Watch/Americas (1994: 2).

[124] The text of the report appeared in *Perfil de la Jornada* (23 Feb. 1994, pp. i-iii).

[125] *Multinational Monitor* (Jan.-Feb. 1994, p. 9).

[126] *Justicia y Paz* (Jan.-March 1994, p. 45). Human Rights Watch/ Americas (1994: 26) was also critical of the CNDH.

CHAPTER 3

[127] *El Financiero* (2 Jan. 1994) quoted García Villalobos (p. 17) and a similar conciliatory statement by the Social Coordination Agency of the state of Chiapas (p. 16).

[128] *Proceso* (10 Jan. 1994, p. 17).

[129] *El Financiero* (3 Jan. 1994, p. 47).

[130] *El Financiero* (5 Jan. 1994, p. 39).

[131] *Uno más Uno* (4 Jan. 1994, p. 1).

[132] *El Financiero* (6 Jan. 1994, p. 34).

[133] *La Jornada* (6 Jan. 1994, p. 7).

[134] Huchim (1994: 307).

[135] *El Financiero* (8 Jan. 1994, p. 13).

[136] *Excélsior* (9 Jan. 1994, p. 1A).

[137] *Excélsior* (9 Jan. 1994, Sec. I, Pt. 3, pp. 2-3).

[138] *Proceso* (24 Jan. 1994, p. 7).

[139] *Reforma* (17 Jan. 1994, p. 1A).

[140] *Proceso* (10 Jan. 1994, p. 16).

[141] *Proceso* (24 Jan. 1994, p. 46).

[142] Cleaver (1994: 21) & Ross (1994: 134).

[143] *Excélsior* (3 March 1994, p. 46A).

[144] *La Jornada* (11 Jan. 1994, p. 14).

[145] Romero Jacobo (1994a: 198).

[146] *El Financiero* (11 Jan. 1994, p. 40).
[147] *El Financiero* (13 Jan. 1994, p. 44).
[148] *Proceso* (24 Jan. 1994, p. 9).
[149] *Perfil de la Jornada* (18 Jan. 1994, p. ii).
[150] *La Jornada* (14 Jan. 1994, p. 7).
[151] *Gaceta de Solidaridad* (15 Jan. 1994, p. 17).
[152] Zea (1994: 32-39).
[153] *CEMOS Memoria* (Feb. 1994, pp. 15-16).
[154] *El Financiero* (21 Jan. 1994, p. 39).
[155] *La Jornada* (23 Jan. 1994, p. 8).
[156] *El Financiero* (3 Jan. 1994, p. 48).
[157] *Reforma* (12 Jan. 1994, p. 6A).
[158] *El Financiero* (3 Jan. 1994, p. 48).
[159] *Reforma* (5 Jan. 1994, p. 7A).
[160] *El Financiero* (2 Jan. 1994, p. 17).
[161] *Reforma* (7 Jan. 1994, p. 8A).

CHAPTER 4

[162] Hernández Navarro (1994d: 6).
[163] Hernández Navarro (1994a: 47).
[164] Harvey (1994b: 29) & *Proceso* (28 Feb. 1994, pp. 6-10).
[165] *La Jornada* (7 Jan. 1994, p. 6).
[166] García de León (1994: I, 95), Harvey (1994b: 30) & *The Other Side of Mexico* (Jan.-Feb. 1994, p. 7).
[167] García de León (1994: II, 229).
[168] Hernández Navarro (1994c: 4).
[169] Harvey (1994b: 30-31).
[170] Many Mexicans, unwilling to closely examine the status quo, simply blame outside organizers for the uprising. If leftist organizers possessed the power to create uprisings, there would have been one in the 1920s and 1930s, a period during which many other leftist organizers entered Chiapas (García de León: 1994: II, 187-99).
[171] *Proceso* (21 Feb. 1994, pp. 9-10).
[172] *The Other Side of Mexico* (Jan.-Feb. 1994, p. 8) and Camú Urzúa & Tótoro Taulis (1994: 25).
[173] The *Christian Science Monitor* (14 Jan. 1994, p. 16).
[174] Tamayo Flores-Alatorre (1994: 41).
[175] *Macrópolis* (31 Jan. 1994: 46).
[176] *Gaceta de Solidaridad* (15 Jan. 1994, p. 5).
[177] *El Financiero* (7 Jan. 1994, p. 34) & Camú Urzúa & Tótoro Taulis (1994: 24).
[178] *Macrópolis* (31 Jan. 1994, pp. 24-25).
[179] Del Muro (1994: 16).
[180] Harvey (1994b: 33).
[181] Harvey (1994b: 32).
[182] *La Jornada del Campo* (25 Jan. 1994, p. 3).
[183] Del Muro (1994: 16).
[184] Harvey (1994b: 35).

[185] Hernández Navarro (1994a: 50).

[186] *Proceso* (24 Jan. 1994, p. 21).

[187] Hernández Navarro (1994b: xxvi) and Camú Urzúa & Tótoro Taulis (1994: 53).

[188] Harvey (1994b: 35).

[189] *Proceso* (10 Jan. 1994, p. 27 & 7 Feb. 1994, p. 11).

[190] *Proceso* (12 April 1993, pp. 6-9; 7 June 1993, pp. 18-21; 23 Aug. 1993, pp. 14-16 & 13 Sept. 1993, pp. 12-15) reported guerrilla activity.

[191] *Proceso* (7 Feb. 1994, p. 11) published the statement, which was issued before the uprising.

[192] *Proceso* (10 Jan. 1994, p. 53) & (21 Feb. 1994, p. 8).

[193] *Village Voice* (1 Feb. 1994, p. 27).

[194] Zea (1994: 15-16).

CHAPTER 5

[195] *La Jornada* (4 Jan. 1994, p. 14).

[196] *El Financiero* (2 Jan. 1994, p. 16—emphasis in original).

[197] *El Financiero International* (10 Jan. 1994, p. 14).

[198] *Excélsior* (17 March 1994, p. 1A).

[199] *Excélsior* (16 Jan. 1994, p. 10A).

[200] *Perfil de la Jornada* (18 Jan. 1994, pp. iii-iv).

[201] *Proceso* (21 Feb. 1994, p. 14).

[202] *Excélsior* (23 Jan. 1994, p. 4A).

[203] *El Financiero International* (21 Feb. 1994, p. 12).

[204] *Proceso* (14 Feb. 1994, p. 50).

[205] Harvey (1994b: 1, 28).

[206] Gómez (1994: 33).

[207] *Excélsior* (16 Jan. 1994, p. 10A).

[208] Guillermoprieto (1994: 53-54).

[209] Romero Jacobo (1994b: 79).

[210] Hernández Castillo (1994: 36-37).

[211] Editorial Collective (1994: 304).

[212] Huchim (1994: 301-02).

[213] Editorial Collective (1994: 302).

[214] Camú Urzúa & Tótoro Taulis (1994: 10, 39, 64).

[215] Camú Urzúa & Tótoro Taulis (1994: 40-41).

[216] *Proceso* (14 Feb. 1994, p. 50) quoted the Indian.

[217] Romero Jacobo (1994b: 125).

[218] The *Los Angeles Times* (17 July 1994, p. 4A).

[219] Gosner (1992: 140).

[220] Editorial Collective (1994: 293).

[221] *Proceso* (7 March 1994, p. 13).

[222] *Proceso* (14 Feb. 1994, p. 25 & 21 Feb. 1994, p. 12).

[223] Camú Urzúa & Tótoro Taulis (1994: 62-65) & Ross (1994: 85).

[224] Trejo Delarbre (1994: 27-28). The photo appeared in *Newsweek* (17 Jan. 1994, p. 27).

[225] *Village Voice* (1 Feb. 1994, p. 28).

[226] *Reforma* (6 Jan. 1994, p. 8A).
[227] *Proceso* (21 Feb. 1994, p. 12).
[228] *El Financiero* (2 March 1994, p. 52).
[229] *Excélsior* (19 Jan. 1994, p. 10A).
[230] Huchim (1994: 303).
[231] Weinberg (l994: p. 56—emphasis in original).
[232] *Justicia y Paz* (Jan.-March 1994, p. 57).
[233] Camú Urzúa & Tótoro Taulis (1994: 71).
[234] *Proceso* (24 Jan. 1994, p. 20).
[235] *Village Voice* (1 Feb. 1994, p. 27).
[236] *Proceso* (24 Jan. 1994, p. 47).
[237] Hernández Navarro (1994a: 44).
[238] *Proceso* (10 Jan. 1994, p. 50).

CHAPTER 6

[239] *Morning Edition* (2 Feb. 1994, p. 9 [transcript]).
[240] *Proceso* (17 Jan. 1994, p. 17).
[241] The *Washington Post* (30 Jan. 1994, p. A30).
[242] The *Washington Post* (3 Feb. 1994, p. A22).
[243] *Proceso* (21 Feb. 1994, p. 30).
[244] *Perfil de la Jornada* (18 Jan. 1994, p. ii).
[245] *La Jornada* (19 Jan. 1994, p. 5).
[246] Ross (1994: 102).
[247] Weinberg (1994: 56).
[248] *This Week with David Brinkley* (9 Jan. 1994, p. 4 [transcript]).
[249] Human Rights Watch/Americas (1994: 24).
[250] The *Journal of Commerce* (14 Jan. 1994, p. 2A).

CHAPTER 7

[251] The *Economist* (22 Jan. 1994, p. 13).
[252] *Proceso* (10 Jan. 1994, p. 60).
[253] *Excélsior* (3 March 1994, pp. 1A, 26A).
[254] Huchim (1994: 311).
[255] *Reforma* (11 Jan. 1994, p. 12A).
[256] *La Jornada* (19 Jan. 1994, p. 6).
[257] Urbina Nandayapa (1994: 114).
[258] *Comercio Exterior* (March 1994, p. 272).
[259] *Reforma* (16 Feb. 1994, p. 1A).
[260] *Excélsior* (3 March 1994, p. 51A).
[261] *El Financiero International* (14 March 1994, p. 12).
[262] *Excélsior* (2 March 1994, p. 39A), *Macrópolis* (7 March 1994, p. 10) & *El Financiero* (17 July 1994, p. 31).
[263] *Macrópolis* (7 March 1994, p. 18).
[264] *El Financiero International* (14 Feb. 1994, p. 1).
[265] *Excélsior* (5 March 1994, p. 29A).
[266] *La Jornada* (15 Jan. 1994, p. 6).

[267] *La Jornada* (30 Jan. 1994, p. 13).
[268] *La Jornada* (3 Feb. 1994, p. 15).
[269] *La Jornada* (23 Feb. 1994, p. 14).
[270] *Proceso* (28 Feb. 1994, p. 22).
[271] Romero Jacobo (1994a: 207).
[272] *El Financiero* (9 March 1994, p. 50).
[273] *Reforma* (10 June 1994, p. 6A).
[274] Urbina Nandayapa (1994: 143).
[275] Romero Jacobo (1994b: 103).
[276] Guillermoprieto (1994: 61).
[277] Huchim (1994: 40).
[278] *Proceso* (21 Feb. 1994, pp. 16-23) & *Punto* (21 Feb. 1994, p. 14) described the release.
[279] Bolívar & Méndez (1994a: 76).
[280] Huchim (1994: 440) & Human Rights Watch/Americas (1994: 9-10).
[281] The *New York Times* (27 Feb. 1994, Sec. 4, p. 5).
[282] Hernández Castillo (1994: 37).
[283] The *New York Times* (Feb. 9, 1994, p. A1) & *Excélsior* (2 March 1994, p. 39A).
[284] The *Washington Post* (10 Feb. 1994, p. A18).
[285] *Reforma* (16 Feb. 1994, p. 5A).
[286] *Proceso* (7 Feb. 1994, p. 12).
[287] *La Jornada* (23 Feb. 1994, p. 9).
[288] The *Christian Science Monitor* (3 March 1994, p. 7).
[289] Harvey (1994b: 26).
[290] *La Jornada* (26 Feb. 1994, p. 9).
[291] The *Washington Post* (22 Feb. 1994, p. A8).
[292] *El Financiero* (18 March 1994, p. 65).
[293] *La Jornada* (26 Feb. 1994, p. 12) & *El Financiero* (18 March 1994, p. 65).
[294] Gómez (1994: 33).
[295] *La Jornada* (21 Feb. 1994, p. 12).
[296] Bolívar & Méndez (1994b: 70) & *El Financiero* (11 Feb. 1994, p. 41).
[297] *Proceso* (14 Feb. 1994, p. 36).
[298] *El Financiero* (13 Jan. 1994, p. 46) & *La Jornada* (13 Jan. 1994, p. 8).
[299] *Proceso* (10 Jan. 1994, p. 8).

CHAPTER 8

[300] *Macrópolis* (7 March 1994, p. 27).
[301] *Proceso* (17 Jan. 1994, p. 11).
[302] *Proceso* (24 Jan. 1994, p. 41).
[303] *La Jornada* (30 Jan. 1994, p. 14).
[304] The *Economist* (19 Feb. 1994, p. 43).
[305] *Reforma* (12 Feb. 1994, p. 1A).
[306] *La Jornada* (23 Feb. 1994, p. 6).
[307] This list is summarized from the description of the accords appearing in *Macrópolis* (7 March 1994, pp. 32-35).
[308] *Reforma* (10 June 1994, p. 6A).

[309] Urbina Nandayapa (1994: 106).
[310] *Macrópolis* (7 March 1994, p. 31).
[311] *El Financiero* (5 March 1994, p. 12).

CHAPTER 9

[312] *Excélsior* (5 March 1994, p. 28A).
[313] The *New York Times* (18 March 18, 1994, p. A3).
[314] *Excélsior* (10 March 1994, p. 26A), *El Financiero* (9 March 1994, p. 49), Urbina Nandayapa (1994: 126) & *El Financiero International* (9 May, 1994, p. 6).
[315] *Proceso* (28 March 1994, p. 33).
[316] *Proceso* (28 March 1994, pp. 32-33).
[317] *La Jornada* (11 April 1994, p. 15).
[318] *La Jornada* (11 April 1994, p. 6).
[319] *Proceso* (18 April 1994, pp. 28-30).
[320] *Proceso* (18 April 1994, p. 31) & *La Jornada* (17 June 1994 p. 17).
[321] The *Austin American-Statesman* (12 April 1994, p. A6).
[322] *La Jornada* (19 June 1994, p. 6).
[323] *Mira* (18 July 1994, pp. 11-12) & Harvey (1994a: 8).
[324] *La Jornada* (31 May 1994, p. 10).
[325] *La Jornada* (16 July 1994, p. 6).
[326] *La Jornada* (13 May 1994, p. 52).
[327] *Reforma* (27 April 1994, p. 5A).
[328] *La Jornada* (28 May 1994, p. 15). After a 65-day sit-in, the mayor of Villa las Rosas was ousted in July (*La Jornada*, 21 July 1994, p. 13).
[329] *El Financiero* (2 May 1994, pp. 77-78).
[330] *Excélsior* (7 July 1994, p. 1A).
[331] *San Antonio Express-News* (28 May 1994, p. 8A).
[332] *La Jornada* (9 May 1994, p. 4).
[333] *Excélsior* (29 March 1994, p. 27A).
[334] *La Jornada* (11 March 1994, p. 12).
[335] *Country Report* (1st quarter 1994, p. 5).
[336] *Excélsior* (17 May 1994, p. 35A).

CHAPTER 10

[337] *La Jornada* (15 June 1994, p. 8).
[338] *El Financiero* (11 March 1994, p. 40).
[339] *Reforma* (11 March 1994, p. 1A).
[340] *La Jornada* (19 March 1994, p. 3).
[341] Guillermoprieto (1994: 60).
[342] *El Financiero* (31 May 1994, p. 53).
[343] *La Jornada* (12 June 1944, p. 3— emphasis in original).
[344] *La Jornada* (17 June 1994, p. 3).
[345] *La Jornada* (13 June 1994, p. 8).
[346] *La Jornada* (13 June 1994, p. 3).
[347] *La Jornada* (14 June 1994, p. 7).

[348] *La Jornada* (13 June 1994, p. 10).
[349] *La Jornada* (13 June 1994, p. 10).
[350] *La Jornada* (16 June 1994, p. 15).
[351] *Excélsior* (15 June 1994, pp. 1F, 7F).
[352] *La Jornada* (17 June 1994, p. 13).
[353] *La Jornada* (17 June 1994, p. 14).
[354] *La Jornada* (13 June 1994, p. 7).
[355] *Excélsior* (18 June 1994, p. 1A).
[356] Camú Urzúa & Tótoro Taulis (1994: 114).

CHAPTER 11

[357] *Reforma* (3 July 1994, p. 7A).
[358] Guillermoprieto (1994: 53).
[359] Harvey (1994a: 8).
[360] *La Jornada* (20 Sept. 1994, p. 13).
[361] *Excélsior* (4 July 1994, p. 42A).
[362] *La Jornada* (1 Aug. 1994, p. 1).
[363] Harvey (1994a: 10).
[364] Harvey (1994a: 8).
[365] *La Jornada* (30 Aug. 1994, p. 18).
[366] *Excélsior* (21 June 1994, p. 5A).
[367] García de León (1985: II, 211).
[368] *Excélsior* (11 Aug. 1994, p. 28A & 10 Sept. 1994, p. 32A), *La Jornada* (10 Sept. 1994, p. 16) & *Proceso* (12 Sept. 1994, p. 36).
[369] *Excélsior* (15 June 1994, p. 33A) & *La Jornada* (21 June 1994, p. 13).
[370] *Excélsior* (30 June 1994, p. 38A).
[371] *La Jornada* (25 June 1994, p. 56 & 11 Sept. 1994, p. 12 & 7 Oct. 1994, p. 16).
[372] *Excélsior* (20 July 1994, p. 28A).
[373] *Proceso* (19 Sept. 1994, p. 39).
[374] The *Dallas Morning News* (4 July 1994, p. 12A).
[375] *Reforma* (8 July 1994, p. 4A).
[376] *La Jornada* (20 Sept. 1994, p. 12).
[377] *La Jornada* (21 Sept. 1994, p. 14).
[378] *Excélsior* (29 July 1994, p. 5A).
[379] *Excélsior* (7 July 1994, p. 38A & 8 July 1994, p. 43A).
[380] The *Washington Post* (6 July 1994, p. 1A).
[381] *La Jornada* (15 Sept. 1994, p. 10).
[382] *La Jornada* (5 Sept. 1994, p. 20).
[383] *Excélsior* (27 May 1994, p. 28A).
[384] *La Jornada* (5 Sept. 1994, p. 20).
[385] *La Jornada* (5 Sept. 1994, p. 20).
[386] *La Jornada* (5 Sept. 1994, p. 20).
[387] *La Jornada* (5 Sept. 1994, p. 20).
[388] *La Jornada* (5 Sept. 1994, p. 20).
[389] *La Jornada* (5 Sept. 1994, p. 20).
[390] *La Jornada* (5 Sept. 1994, p. 20).

[391] *Excélsior* (8 Aug. 1994, p. 16A).

[392] *La Jornada* (5 Sept. 1994, p. 20).

[393] *La Jornada* (1 Oct. 1994, p. 14).

[394] *La Jornada* (12 June 1994, p. 23).

[395] *La Jornada* (15 Sept. 1994, p. 12).

[396] *Excélsior* (8 July 1994, p. 47A).

[397] *La Jornada* (17 Oct. 1994, p. 9).

[398] *Excélsior* (3 Aug. 1994, p. 1A) & *El Financiero* (3 Aug. 1994, p. 21).

[399] *El Financiero* (2 Aug. 1994, p. 41).

[400] *La Jornada* (3 July 1994, p. 3—emphasis in original).

[401] The groups were listed in *Reforma* (6 Aug. 1994, p. 4A & 11 Aug. 1994, p. 2A), *El Financiero* (15 Aug. 1994, p. 14), *Proceso* (1 Aug. 1994, p. 7 & 15 Aug. 1994, p. 24) & *La Jornada* (18 Aug. 1994, p. 18).

[402] *El Financiero* (8 Aug. 1994, p. 61).

[403] *Excélsior* (10 Aug. 1994, pp. 43A, 47A) & *Perfil de la Jornada* (20 Aug. 1994, pp. i-iii).

[404] *Excélsior* (11 Aug. 1994, p. 35A).

[405] *La Jornada* (2 Aug. 1994, p. 12).

[406] *Reforma* (3 Aug. 1994, p. 7A).

[407] *Proceso* (8 Aug. 1994, p. 9).

[408] *El Financiero* (10 Aug. 1994, p. 44).

[409] *El Financiero International* (15 Aug. 1994, p. 14).

[410] *El Financiero International* (15 Aug. 1994, p. 14).

[411] Lagunes (1994: 24-25).

[412] *Reforma* (2 Aug. 1994, p. 9A).

[413] *Reforma* (12 Aug. 1994, p. 7A).

[414] Camú Urzúa & Tótoro Taulis (1994: 137).

[415] *El Financiero* (7 Aug. 1994, p. 5).

[416] *El Financiero* (2 Aug. 1994, p. 41).

[417] Excluded media were listed in *Reforma* (6 Aug. 1994, p. 1A) & *Excélsior* (7 Aug. 1994, p. 31A). They included Televisa, TV Azteca, the newspapers *Summa, Novedades*, *La Prensa,* and *Ovaciones,* the magazines *Epoca* and *Siempre,* and Radio Red de Chiapas.

[418] *Reforma* (22 Aug. 1994, p. 2A).

[419] *La Jornada* (26 July 1994, p. 7).

[420] *Reforma* (14 Aug. 1994, p. 6A).

[421] *Últimas Noticias* [2nd ed.] (17 Aug. 1994, p. 6).

[422] *El Financiero* (20 Sept. 1994, p. 46).

[423] *La Jornada* (9 Sept. 1994, p. 18).

[424] *El Financiero* (5 May 1994, p. 30).

[425] *La Jornada* (15 June 1994, p. 18).

[426] Hernández Navarro (1994e: 2).

[427] *Reforma* (24 Aug. 1994, p. 1A). In addition to the comments cited in the text, negative evaluations of the elections in Chiapas appeared in *La Jornada* (5 Oct. 1994, p. 24 & 15 Oct. 1994, p. 15), *El Financiero* (25 Oct. 1994, p. 52), and *Proceso* (7 Nov. 1994, pp. 12-19).

[428] *La Jornada* (31 Aug. 1994, p. 12).

[429] *Proceso* (19 Sept. 1994, p. 9).

[430] Ross (1994: 391).
[431] *La Jornada* (28 Aug. 1994, p. 11).
[432] *Proceso* (19 Sept. 1994, p. 41).
[433] The *Dallas Morning News* (27 Aug. 1994, p. 24A).
[434] *Proceso* (29 Aug. 1994, p. 18).
[435] *La Jornada* (26 Sept. 1994, p. 7).
[436] *La Jornada* (31 Aug. 1994, p. 5).
[437] *La Joranda* (8 Sept. 1994, p. 1).
[438] *La Jornada* (5 Sept. 1994, p. 1).
[439] *El Financiero* (2 July 1994, p. 16).
[440] *La Jornada* (20 Sept. 1994, p. 13).
[441] *Reforma* (21 July 1994, p. 6A).
[442] The *New York Times* (18 Sept. 1994, p. 8).
[443] *La Jornada* (11 Oct. 1994, p. 14).
[444] *Proceso* (24 Oct. 1994, p. 16).
[445] *Proceso* (24 Oct. 1994, p. 14).
[446] *Proceso* (24 Oct. 1994, p. 15).
[447] *La Jornada* (12 Oct. 1994, p. 12).
[448] *La Jornada* (14 Oct. 1994, p. 18).
[449] *El Financiero International* (17 Oct. 1994, p. 3).
[450] *El Financiero International* (24 Oct. 1994, p. 3).
[451] *La Jornada* (2 Nov. 1994, p. iii).
[452] The *New York Times* (19 Oct. 1994, p. A6).
[453] *Proceso* (17 Oct. 1994, p. 18).
[454] *Proceso* (17 Oct. 1994, p. 38).
[455] *Proceso* (17 Oct. 1994, p. 39).
[456] *La Jornada* (4 Oct. 1994, p. 20).
[457] *El Norte* (20 Oct. 1994, p. 8A).
[458] *Proceso* (31 Oct. 1994, p. 24).
[459] Descriptions of the San Cristóbal rally appeared in the *Austin Chronicle* (4 Nov. 1994, p. 15), *El Financiero International* (17 Oct. 1994, p. 3), *Proceso* (17 Oct. 1994, p. 39), and *La Jornada* (13 Oct. 1994, pp. 11-15).
[460] *El Norte* (20 Oct. 1994, p. 8A).
[461] *Proceso* (31 Oct. 1994, p. 23).
[462] *La Jornada* (7 Nov. 1994, p. 20).
[463] The *New York Times* (18 Sept. 1994, p. 8).
[464] The *Austin American-Statesman* (4 July 1994, p. 16A).
[465] Reygadas *et al.* (1994: 8-9).
[466] *La República* (12 May 1994, pp. 12-13).
[467] *Proceso* (1 Aug. 1994, p. 11).

CHAPTER 12

[468] *La Jornada* (17 June 1994, p. 6).
[469] *La Jornada* (26 Jan. 1994, p. 10).
[470] *La Jornada* (15 June 1994, p. 12).
[471] *La Jornada* (29 July 1994, p. 18).
[472] *La Jornada* (13 June 1994, p. 15).

[473] The *Wall Street Journal* (18 Feb. 1994, p. A15).
[474] *Uno más Uno* (Feb. 16, 1994, p. 5).
[475] *El Financiero International* (28 March 1994, p. 16).
[476] *La Jornada* (31 Jan. 1994, p. 6).
[477] *El Financiero* (13 Feb. 1994, p. 5).
[478] Harvey (1994b: 37).
[479] The *Journal of Commerce* (20 Jan. 1994, p. 8A).
[480] *Proceso* (7 March 1994, p. 21).
[481] Romero Jacobo (1994b: 93).
[482] *Gaceta de Solidaridad* (15 Jan. 1994, p. 4).
[483] *Ojarasca* (June-July 1994, p. 10).
[484] Méndez Asenio & Cano Gimeno (1994: 48).
[485] Nigh (1994: 9).
[486] Bartra (1984: 2).
[487] The *Los Angeles Times* (23 Feb. 1994, p. A4).
[488] The *Los Angeles Times* (23 Feb. 1994, p. A4).
[489] Ross (1994: 265).
[490] Bardach (1994: 132).
[491] *El Financiero International* (28 March 1994, p. 16).
[492] Medina (1994: 12).
[493] Collier (1994: 15).
[494] Cancian & Brown (1994: 25).

Abbreviations:

ANCIEZ: Emiliano Zapata Independent National Peasant Alliance.

ARIC: Rural Association of Collective Interest, a peasant confederation usually allied with the PRI.

CCRI: Clandestine Indian Revolutionary Committee.

CEOIC: State Council of Indigenous and Peasant Organizations, a major confederation organized in January 1994.

CIOAC: Independent Farmworkers and Peasants Central, a confederation which began organizing coffee workers in the mid-1970s.

CNC: National Peasant Confederation, the government-sponsored peasant organization.

CND: National Democratic Convention.

CNDH: National Commission for Human Rights, a government agency created in 1990 to address the problem of human-rights abuse.

CONASUPO: National Company for People's Sustenance.

EZLN: Zapatista Army of National Liberation, the name chosen by the group which rebelled in Chiapas.

INI: National Indigenous Institute, a government agency which addresses problems of Mexico's indigenous population.

MRE: Meals Ready to Eat, rations supplied to troops in the field.

NAFTA: North American Free Trade Agreement.

OCEZ: Emiliano Zapata Peasant Organization.

PAN: National Action Party, a political party founded in 1939. Traditionally the No. 2 party, with conservative ideology.

PRD: Party of the Democratic Revolution, the party closely associated with Cuauhtémoc Cárdenas. Founded in 1990, the party is generally characterized as center-left.

PRI: Party of the Institutionalized Revolution. This party, founded in 1929, has dominated political life since.

Cast of Characters:

Avendaño, Amado: co-editor of the San Cristóbal newspaper *Tiempo*, and 1994 PRD gubernatorial candidate in Chiapas.

Camacho Solís, Manuel: appointed as mayor of Mexico City by President Salinas in 1988, he was seen as a likely PRI candidate for the 1994-2000 presidential term. However, he was passed over by Salinas, who later appointed him as peace commissioner.

Cárdenas, Cuauhtémoc: 1994 PRD presidential candidate, son of President Lázaro Cárdenas, who served as president 1934-1940.

Castellanos Domínguez, Absalón: governor of Chiapas, 1982-88, a period during which there was widespread repression against Indians. In his classic book on Mexico, *Distant Neighbors*, Alan Riding stated that the governor had identified his three major enemies as the National Indigenous Institute, the diocese of San Cristóbal, and doctors in Comitán who provided medical assistance to Guatemalan refugees.

Colosio, Luis: the original 1984 PRI presidential candidate. He was assassinated in Tijuana on 23 March 1994.

Constantino Kanter, Jorge: most prominent spokesman for the Chiapan cattlemen.

Díaz, Porfirio: president (and dictator) of Mexico, 1876-1911, toppled by the Mexican Revolution.

González Garrido, Patrocinio: governor of Chiapas, 1988-1993, Interior Minister, 1993-1994. Writing in 1992, Adolfo Aguilar Zinzer declared: "He is a petty tyrant, capable of great abuses and injustice. Not many governors in Mexico deserve such a title, but Patrocinio does."

Ibarra de Piedra, Rosario: human-rights activist and former presidential candidate, selected as president of the National Democratic Convention.

López Moreno, Javier: replaced Elmar Setzer as governor of Chiapas in January 1994.

Madrazo, José: Manuel Camacho Solís' replacement as government peace negotiator.

"Marcos": nom de guerre of the rebel subcommander who became a media sensation, serving as spokesperson for EZLN. One of the organizers who arrived in Chiapas in 1983 and later died there was named Marcos. The current "Marcos" adopted his name.

Robledo, Eduardo: 1994 PRI gubernatorial candidate in Chiapas.

Ruiz, Samuel: born in Irapuato, Guanajuato, in 1924, he was consecrated bishop in 1960. In 1968, he attended the Conference of Latin American Bishops in Medellín, Columbia, a seminal event in liberation theology. In *Distant Neighbors*, Riding described him as one of the bishops who "have long been identified with Indian interests, channeling outside assistance to them and denouncing to the rest of the country the repression and exploitation they suffer." In 1993, Ruiz published a 30-page summary of conditions in Chiapas. The report noted, "Poor people who demand their rights through legal channels are repressed. Middlemen speculate in products of the countryside. Jails are full of innocent people. Hunger and malnutrition are a permanent fact of life for many indigenous." In 1993, he received the Letelier-Moffitt Human Rights Award. After the rebellion, he was chosen as mediator for negotiations between the government and the EZLN. For his positions, before and after the rebellion, he has been subject to vitriolic attacks from conservatives.

Salinas de Gortari, Carlos: president of Mexico (1988 to 1994). Salinas received a Ph.D. from Harvard and then began a career working in the Mexican government. His claimed electoral victory over Cuauhtémoc Cárdenas in 1988 is widely seen as tainted by fraud. He served as secretary of budget and planning from 1982 to 1987, and thus for 12 years was a key architect of Mexican economic policy.

Setzer, Elmar: a prosperous cattleman who served as interim governor, replacing González Garrido in 1993. Setzer was then replaced early in 1994. He and many land-owning families in Chiapas are descended from German families who settled in Chiapas to grow coffee during the Díaz administration.

Zapata, Emiliano: Zapata led peasant revolutionaries in the central Mexico state of Morelos from 1910 to 1919. He was killed in an ambush laid by the rival forces of Venustiano Carranza. The slogan "land and liberty" is associated with his movement.

Zedillo, Ernesto: the victorious PRI presidential candidate designated in 1994 to replace the assassinated Colosio. He received a Ph.D. in economics from Yale. During the Salinas administration, he served as secretary of planning and budget and as secretary of education. At his 1 December 1994, inauguration, he spoke of "the conditions of profound injustice, misery, and neglect which led to violence" in Chiapas. Zedillo then noted he still placed his hopes on negotiation to achieve a dignified, just peace and pledged his government would not initiate violence.

GLOSSARY

cacique: a local boss who controls many aspects of political and economic life and who enjoys wide-ranging impunity from criminal prosecution.

caciquismo: government by caciques.

catechist: lay teacher often associated with liberation theology in Chiapas.

campesino: peasant.

caudillo: an insurgent leader.

Chol: one of the smaller Mayan groups in Chiapas.

científicos: advisors to Porfirio Díaz who introduced what they considered "scientific" economic policy.

compañero/compañera: the male and female forms of the word for comrade, or fellow member of a rebel group.

criollos: people of European ancestry born in the New World.

Declaration of the Lacandón Rain Forest: the initial announcement of the EZLN's existence, which declared war on the Mexican government and stated the EZLN's goals. It became known as the First Declaration of the Lacandón Rain Forest, after the publication of a second document in June, which called for the holding of the National Democratic Convention. This latter document, called the Second Declaration of the Lacandón Rain Forest, declared, "The EZLN will consider the Democratic National Convention as the authentic representative of the interests of the Mexican people in its transition to democracy."

ejido: land distributed via the land reform. Until recent changes in the constitution, ejido land could be farmed by individuals, but not legally sold or rented. This prohibition was designed to prevent the re-concentration of land ownership. The landless living near estates in excess of the legal size limit could file a claim to the land. If approved by the government, title to the land would revert from the landowners to the government. Those who had filed the claim, and their heirs, could farm the land they had claimed—the ejido—and keep the produce.

Grijalva River: the river draining southern and western Chiapas. The river, a major source of hydroelectric power, drains into the Gulf of Mexico. It is also known as the Río Grande de Chiapas.

Guadalupe Tepeyac: de facto rebel capital, located in eastern Chiapas, east-southeast of San Cristóbal. Aguascalientes, site of the National Democratic Convention, is adjacent.

hacendado: the owner of a large estate, or hacienda.

hectare: the metric unit of land measure, equals 2.47 acres.

Lacandón: the rain forest in eastern Chiapas, bordering the Usumacinta River. This term also refers to the Mayan group living there.

Mam: one of the smaller Mayan groups in Chiapas.

mestizo: a person of mixed Indian and European ancestry.

Mexican Revolution: the social upheaval which began in 1910 to oust dictator Porfirio Díaz. It later saw widespread combat between rival groups with differing visions of how to restructure Mexico. One of its key demands was land reform—the government-mandated division of large estates to provide access to land for the landless.

nixtamal: corn cooked in lime or ash so it can be used to make tortillas.

Pemex: the government-owned oil company.

San Cristóbal de las Casas (or simply, "San Cristóbal"): colonial capital of Chiapas and power center for the indigenous highlands. It is named for the 16th century bishop of Chiapas, Bartolomé de las Casas, an early defender of Indian rights.

Tojolabal: one of the smaller Mayan groups in Chiapas.

Tuxtla Gutiérrez (or simply "Tuxtla"): the state capital of Chiapas since 1892 and the traditional rival of San Cristóbal.

Tzeltal: a Mayan group inhabiting the highlands and northern Chiapas, to the east of the Tzotzils.

Tzotzil: a Mayan group inhabiting the highlands, to the west of the Tzeltals.

Zapatista: a member or sympathizer of the Zapatista National Liberation Army.

Zoque: an Indian group from western Chiapas.

Appendix I: Statistical Data for Chiapas

Jobs in primary sector (includes agriculture, cattle, forestry, fishing, and hunting): 52.9%[1]

Illiteracy rate in population older than 15: 30.0% (for all of Mexico, 12.4%)[2]

Percent of illiterate adults who are women: 63%[3]

Population in 1990: 3,210,496[4]

Population without electricity: 34.9% (for all of Mexico, 13.0%)[5]

Population living in localities of fewer than 2,000: 56.9%[6]

Population older than 15 with less than primary education: 62.08%[7]

Working population receiving more than one minimum wage: 41.1% (for all of Mexico, 73.5%)[8]

Main crops by area planted, as of 1992:[9]

corn	743,525.2 hectares
coffee	231,328.8 hectares
beans	102,498.8 hectares
cacao	30,000.0 hectares
banana	19,952.0 hectares

Total area of state	7,521,044 hectares
ejido area	3,015,277 hectares
private holdings	2,496,471 hectares [10]

---

[1] Bailón (1994: 10).
[2] Pazos (1994: 119).
[3] *Macrópolis* (31 Jan. 1994, p. 34).
[4] *XI Censo de Población y Vivienda 1990*, Vol. 7, Tomo 1, p. 4.
[5] Pazos (1994: 120).
[6] Bailón (1994: 11).
[7] Huchim (1994: 340).
[8] Pazos (1994: 118).
[9] *Macrópolis* (31 Jan. 1994, p. 36).
[10] *Macrópolis* (31 Jan. 1994, p. 26).

Appendix II: Rebel Communiqués

[The initial communiqué of the Zapatista Liberation Army was entitled the "Declaration of the Lacandón Rain Forest." This declaration was posted in San Cristóbal on 1 January 1994 and was the document which introduced the EZLN to the world. There are 10 demands (jobs, land, etc.) in the last paragraph (if "justice and peace" are counted as one). These were widely referred to as the Ten Points. In January, the rebels frequently referred to the Ten Points as their basic set of demands. The emphasis appeared in the original Spanish version.]

Declaration of the Lacandón Rain Forest
Today we say, "Enough is enough!"
To the Mexican people:
To our Mexican brothers and sisters:

We are the product of 500 years of struggle. Our first struggle was against slavery. Then came the War of Independence from Spain, led by the insurgents. After that came the struggle to prevent our being absorbed by U.S. expansionism. Still later we promulgated our constitution and expelled the French imperialists from our soil. Then, after the Díaz dictatorship refused to enforce the laws of the Reform in a just manner, the people rebelled. Villa and Zapata, who were poor men like us, emerged as their leaders.

We have been denied the most elemental education, so they can use us as cannon fodder and pillage the wealth of our country. It does not matter to them that we are dying of hunger and curable diseases. We have nothing, absolutely nothing—not a decent home, no land, no job, no health care, no food, and no education. We don't even have the right to democratically elect our officials. We have neither independence from foreigners nor peace and justice for ourselves and our children.

Today **we say, "Enough is enough!"** We are the descendants of those who forged this nation. We, the dispossessed, number in the millions. We urge our brothers and sisters to heed this call. It is the only way to avoid dying of hunger, given the insatiable greed of the dictatorship. For more than 70 years, this dictatorship has been run by a clique of traitors who represent the most conservative groups which sell out the country. They are the same ones who opposed Hidalgo and Morelos and betrayed Vicente Guerrero. They are the same ones who sold more than half of our nation to the foreign invader. They are the same ones who brought a European prince to govern us. They are the same ones who created the dictatorship led by Díaz' *científicos*. They are the same ones who opposed nationalizing the oil industry.

They are the ones who massacred railroad workers in 1958 and students in 1968. They are the same ones who take everything, absolutely everything, from us today.

To prevent all of this, and as our last hope, after having attempted to exercise the rights guaranteed by our Constitution, we invoke the authority granted by Article 39 of our Constitution, which states:

> National sovereignty resides essentially and originally in the people. The powers of government come from the people and are instituted to benefit them. The citizens have, at all times, the inalienable right to change or modify their form of government.

Thus, based on our constitutional rights, we direct this message to the Mexican army, the foundation of the dictatorship which we suffer under. This one-party dictatorship is led by the illegal head of the executive branch, Carlos Salinas de Gortari.

Based on this declaration of war, we ask that the judicial and legislative branches assume the responsibility of restoring legality and stability to Mexico by deposing the dictator.

We also request that the International Red Cross and other international agencies monitor the combat involving our forces, thus protecting the civilian population. We declare that we are now and always will be subject to the provisions of the Geneva Convention. The EZLN is a true belligerent force engaged in a struggle of liberation. The Mexican people are on our side. We have our homeland, and the tricolor flag, which is loved and respected by the **insurgent** combatants. We use the colors red and black in our uniforms, since they are symbols of working people on strike. Our flag carries the letters EZLN, Zapatista Army of National Liberation. We will always carry it into combat.

We reject beforehand our enemies' attempt to discredit the justice of our cause by referring to us as drug traffickers, narco-guerrillas, bandits, and other such terms. Our struggle is based on constitutional law and has as its goals justice and equality.

Based on this Declaration of War, we are ordering the military forces of the Zapatista Army of National Liberation to:

1) Advance to the national capital, defeating the federal army while protecting the civilian population and permitting those liberated to democratically elect their own authorities.

2) Respect the lives of prisoners and turn the wounded over to the International Red Cross so they can receive medical care.

3) Begin summary treason trials of federal army soldiers and the political police who have been advised, trained, and paid by foreigners, either inside Mexico or abroad. Those repressing or mistreating the civilian population or

robbing or harming the national patrimony will also be charged with treason.

4) Form new military units made up of all Mexicans who are willing to join our just cause, including those enemy soldiers who give up without fighting and promise to follow the orders of the General Command of the **Zapatista Army of National Liberation.**

5) Ask the unconditional surrender of enemy units before engaging in combat.

6) End the pillaging of our natural resources in areas controlled by the EZLN.

To the People of Mexico:

We, free men and women, are conscious that the war we have declared is our last resort. Nevertheless, it is a just action. For many years, the dictators have been waging an undeclared, genocidal war against our people. Thus, we ask your active support of this declaration of the Mexican people, who are struggling for *jobs, land, housing, food, health care, education, independence, liberty, democracy, justice and peace.* We will fight until these basic demands of the Mexican people have been met by the formation of a free, democratic government.

Join the insurgent forces of the Emiliano Zapata Army of National Liberation!

General Command of the EZLN, 1993

◆ ◆ ◆

> [This communiqué of 6 January was issued in response to charges concerning the nature of the EZLN, and especially its alleged ties to other groups. It called for the resignation of Salinas and announced the rebels' conditions for beginning dialogue with the government.]
>
> "Here we are, the dead of all times, dying once again, but now so we can live."

To the Mexican people:
The people and governments of the world:

Brothers and sisters:

On the first of January of this year, our Zapatista troops began a series of political-military actions whose main objective is informing the people of

Mexico and of the world about the miserable conditions under which millions of Mexicans, especially we the indigenous people, live and die. With these actions, we also have shown our willingness to fight for our most basic rights by the only means government authorities have left us—armed struggle.

The appalling poverty of our compatriots has a common cause: the absence of liberty and democracy. We consider that genuine respect for liberty and democracy are absolutely essential for improving the economic and social position of the dispossessed in Mexico. For this reason, we demand freedom and democracy, and call on the illegitimate government of Carlos Salinas to resign. This would permit the formation of a democratic transitional government which would guarantee fair elections throughout the country and at all levels of government. We reaffirm our political and economic demands, and, based on them, we hope to unite the Mexican people and their independent organizations. Thus, through all forms of struggle, a national revolutionary movement can be created. Such a movement would embrace all social organizations which are honestly, patriotically working to improve Mexico.

Since the beginning of our war of national liberation, we have received attacks from repressive government agencies and the federal army. We have also been slandered by the federal and state governments and by some mass media which attempt to fool the Mexican people by denigrating our movement. They say our movement is directed by foreigners, professionals terrorists, sinister, unpatriotic individuals who only seek personal gain. Due to such slander and lies, the EZLN has been forced to declare:

1) There is not a single foreigner in the ranks of the EZLN nor in any leadership position. No foreign revolutionary group has provided support or training, nor has any foreign government. The report that there are Guatemalans in our ranks and that we were trained in that neighboring country are stories concocted by the federal government to discredit our cause. We have had no ties to, nor do we now have any connection with, the Salvadoran FMLN, or with the Guatemalan URNG, or with any other armed movement from Latin America, North America, Europe, Africa, Asia, or Oceania. Our military tactics are drawn not from Central America, but from Mexican military history, from Hidalgo, Morelos, Guerrero, and Mina, from the resistance to the Yankee invasion of 1846-47, from the grass-roots response to the French invasion, from the heroic feats of Villa and Zapata, and from indigenous resistance throughout the history of our country.

2) The EZLN has no ties to the hierarchy of the Catholic Church nor that of any other church. We have not received training or advice from the church hierarchy or from any of the dioceses in Chiapas. Nor have we received any assistance from the papal nuncio, the Vatican, or from anyone. Most of our troops are Catholics, but there are people from other denominations and religions.

3) The officers and troops of the EZLN are mainly Chiapan Indians. This is because we Indians form the most dispossessed, humiliated group in Mexico. However, as can be seen, we are also the most dignified. We Indians have risen in arms by the thousands. Tens of thousands of our family members support us. The government claims that this is not an indigenous rebellion. We, however, feel that if thousands of Indians rebel, it's an Indian rebellion. Mexicans from other states and social origins are also in our movement. They agree with us and they have **joined us** because they oppose the exploitation which we suffer. Other Mexicans will join these non-Indians because our struggle is national and will not be limited to Chiapas. Currently, all of our leaders are Indians. All of the members of the clandestine revolutionary committees are members of such groups as the Tzeltal, Tzotzil, Chol, and Tojolabal. All of the Indians have not sided with us yet, because many of our fellow Indians still accept government lies. However, there are now several thousand of us, and we must be taken into consideration. The use of ski masks and other means to hide our faces results from security considerations and prevents the cult of the individual leader.

4) The arms and equipment of our people are varied. As can be easily understood, they were not all put on public display in the municipal seats which we occupied on 1 and 2 January. Our arms and equipment were gradually gathered and readied during the 10 years during which our forces were secretly training. The "sophisticated" communications gear that we have can be bought at any import shop in Mexico. In order to acquire our arms and equipment, we never resorted to robbery, kidnapping, or extortion. We have always relied on donations made by humble, honest people throughout Mexico. Since we never resorted to banditry, the repressive state security forces never detected us during our 10-year period of careful preparation.

5) Some may wonder why we decided to start now, if we were ready earlier. The reason is that we fruitlessly attempted to exhaust all legal channels. During this 10-year period, more than 150,000 of our Indian brothers and sisters died of curable diseases. The economic and social plans of the municipal, state, and federal governments didn't offer any real solutions to our problems. They just give us handouts at election time. But the handouts only last a little while. Then death returns to our homes. We will no longer tolerate useless deaths. If we die now, it will be with dignity as our forefathers did, not with shame. It's better to fight for change, as our forefathers did. Another 150,000 of us are ready to die if that is what it takes to wake our people up from the deception that has gripped them.

6) The conditions for dialogue which our government wants to impose on us are unacceptable to the EZLN. We will not lay down our arms until the demands we made at the beginning of our struggle have been met. Instead, we propose the following conditions which must be met before negotiations begin:

a) recognition of the EZLN as a belligerent force.

b) a cease-fire by both sides throughout the war zone.

c) withdrawal of all federal troops from occupied communities, with full respect for human rights. Federal troops should be returned to their barracks in other parts of Mexico.

d) an end to indiscriminate bombing of rural areas.

e) the formation of a national mediation committee, once the last three conditions have been met.

Our troops pledge to abide by these conditions, if the federal troops do so. However, if they don't, our troops will continue to advance on the national capital.

The EZLN reaffirms that it is abiding by the laws of war established by the Geneva Convention. It will respect the civilian population, the Red Cross, the press, the wounded, and enemy troops who surrender to us.

We make a special plea to the U.S. people and their government. We call on the U.S. people to show us solidarity and aid our fellow countrymen. We ask the U.S. government to suspend all economic and military aid to the Mexican government because it is a dictatorship which does not respect human rights and because this aid will be used to massacre the Mexican people.

Mexicans: As of 5 January, the military results are as follows:

1) Zapatista casualties: nine dead and 20 seriously wounded who were treated in our field hospitals. An undetermined number suffered minor wounds and returned to their posts. Twelve are missing in action. We have not included in this number our wounded who were cowardly executed in cold blood with a shot to the head by officers of the federal army. The number of these comrades has still not been determined since our troops continue fighting in Ocosingo.

2) Enemy casualties, including police and federal soldiers: 27 dead, 40 wounded, and 180 prisoners who surrendered to our forces and were later freed unharmed. There are at least 30 other unconfirmed deaths in the federal army. These casualties, along with an undetermined number of wounded, occurred on 4 January when Mexican Air Force planes bombed the mountains south of San Cristóbal de las Casas. The bombs fell on army trucks which were in the area.

3) Enemy war material destroyed or damaged includes three helicopter gunships of the Mexican Air Force (one in Ocosingo and two in San Cristóbal), three ground-support aircraft (in San Cristóbal), 15 police cars, 15 trucks, and four torture centers of the State Judicial Police.

4) Freed prisoners: 230 from four jails captured by our forces (two in San Cristóbal, one in Ocosingo, and one in Las Margaritas).

5) Arms captured include 207 weapons of various calibers (M-16, G-3, M-2, grenade launchers, shotguns, and pistols) and an undetermined number of bullets of various calibers.

- 1,266 kilograms of dynamite and 10,000 TNT detonators.
- more than 20 trucks.
- an undetermined number of police, army, and air force radios.

To the national and international press:

We would like to inform the honest national and international press of the genocide being carried out by federal forces in the municipal seats of San Cristóbal, Ocosingo, Altamirano, and Las Margaritas, as well as along nearby highways. They indiscriminately kill civilians and then claim they were killed by the EZLN. Some of the Zapatista army members they claim to have killed are in perfect health. The attitude of the federal troops is in sharp contrast to that of our troops, who are constantly concerned with protecting civilian lives. The civilian population of these towns can serve as witness to this. Most of the damage done to public and private buildings, which was blamed on EZLN troops, was done by federal troops when they entered these four municipal seats.

To the federal army:

The present conflict, once again, unmasks the nature of the federal army and reveals its true essence—indiscriminate repression, violation of all human rights, and the complete lack of ethics and military honor. The murder by federal forces of women and children in combat areas indicates an army out of control. We call on the federal officers and troops to simply refuse to follow orders by superior officers to kill civilians and summarily execute prisoners of war and the wounded. Rather, they should be guided by ethics and military honor. We would again like to extend an invitation to them to desert the ranks of the bad government and join our just cause—the cause of a people who, as you have witnessed, only desire to live in justice or die with dignity. We have respected the lives of the soldiers and police who have surrendered to our forces. You share complicity in summarily executing Zapatistas who surrendered or were wounded and unable to fight. If you begin to attack our families and do not respect the lives of prisoners and the wounded, then we will begin to do the same.

To the Mexican people:

Finally, we would like to call on workers, poor peasants, teachers, students, housewives, professionals, and honest, progressive intellectuals, as well as all independent organizations, to join our struggle wherever you are and to struggle by all possible means until we obtain the justice and liberty we desire for all Mexicans.

We won't lay down our arms!
We want justice, not pardons and handouts!

From the mountains of southeastern Mexico
CCRI-General Command of the EZLN

◆ ◆ ◆

[On 10 April 1994, this communiqué was read to the roughly 50,000 people assembled in the main plaza in Mexico City to commemorate the 75th anniversary of the assassination of Emiliano Zapata.]

Communiqué of the Clandestine Revolutionary Indigenous Committee—General Command of the EZLN, Mexico

10 April 1994

To the Mexican people:
To the peoples and governments of the world:
To the national and international press:
Brothers and sisters:

The Clandestine Revolutionary Committee of the Emiliano Zapata Liberation Front would like to inform you of the following:

Today, 10 April 1994, is the 75th anniversary of the assassination of Gen. Emiliano Zapata. The treachery of Venustiano Carranza tried to stifle his cry—"Land and Liberty!" Today, the usurper Carlos Salinas de Gortari, who calls himself "President of the Republic," lies to the Mexican people when he says that the reforms to Article 27 of the Constitution reflect the spirit of Gen. Zapata. The government lies! Zapata's legacy cannot be eliminated by haughty decrees. Those who work the land have an irrevocable right to it. The battle cry of "Land and liberty" continues to reverberate throughout Mexico. Neo-liberalism darkens the Mexican landscape. Under its guise, all of the peasants who struggle for their land rights are jailed and murdered. Salinas' reforms to Article 27 of the Constitution constitute treason. The person who usurped power in Mexico should be put on trial for this crime.

Brothers and sisters, 100 days ago our voices broke the silence. The voices of landless peasants, of agricultural workers, of small landowners, of Mexican Indians spoke through the muzzles of guns held by faceless men and women. The voices of those who have nothing and deserve everything had to follow the path of its smallest men, its most humiliated, its most persecuted, its most forgotten. It was the voice of genuine men, of Mexicans who have been stripped of their land, of their dignity, of their history. Everything was lost in our peoples' long night. The land only produced despair and death. Ten years ago, some good people sowed in these sorrowful lands the hope that once again true men would return to life. The seed of their action found fertile ground in the Mexican mountains. Their silence began to grow. The night gave way to dawn.

After they proclaimed, "Enough is enough," the land bore fruit of this seed. Despair was transformed into rage. Instead of humiliation, there was dignity. Instead of laments, they harvested guns. Thousands of men and women dug from the very soil which had only given them poverty, that which would fill their hands, which would cover their faces, and wipe out their past. They left behind their identities and their land and marched off to battle. None of us, men and women who walk at night, will have a tomorrow. We can never leave behind our anxieties. There will be no rest for our bones and our blood.

Why are these men and women on the move? Who drinks their blood? For whom are their words? Who will receive life from their death? One hundred days. Ten years. Which of you will take up the flag they snatched from the rich with their blood? Who will follow their steps along the path of dignity? Who, in addition to us, who are just a glance, a voice and unrestrained tenderness, will speak? Who will shout with us? Who will not abandon us? Who will struggle with us? Who will listen to our dead?

Not the usurper, who haughtily rules in the National Palace. Not he who sells us out. Not he who murders us. Not he who rips us off. Not he who humiliates us.

You, brothers and sisters. For you, our blood. Our pale light dispels everyone's night. For your life, our deaths. Our war is for your peace. Our words are for your ears. Brothers and sisters, your pain will be alleviated by our struggle. For you, everything, brothers and sisters, for us, nothing.

Brothers and sisters, in front of you, in the National Palace, deceit rules supreme. The person living there, whom no person of good will wanted to be there, denies us everything. The powerful master who snatches life itself from us every day should leave. He must go. His voice should not control us. Nothing good will emerge from those doors. There are lies on his face and deceit in his words. He must go. This is the message which comes from the mountains, this is what our blood says, this is what our dead ask. He must go. Brothers and sisters, tell him that! He must go!

Let no one else occupy the Palace, which is in front of you, without having popular support. He who sits in the presidential chair should govern obeying the people. He who speaks from the balcony should tell the truth. He who is our leader should obey us. Tell them, brothers and sisters, this is what we want.

Brothers and sisters, we cannot be with you today. Our footsteps continue in the dark of the mountains, our voice distant and muzzled. Take up our call. Let us use your voice for a moment, so that it can speak our words. At this very moment, in the mountains of southeast Mexico, thousands of men and women, with their faces covered, who have no name and no past, are filling their lungs with the battle cry of the first of January. Our heart is happy, since once again, with your steps, Emiliano Zapata is walking into the main plaza of Mexico City. Our small, forgotten group will raise the image of Zapata in the other heart of the nation, that of the mountains of southeast Mexico.

Greetings, Mexican brothers and sisters! May our cry be yours!
Who will struggle with us? Who will listen to our dead?
Long live Emiliano Zapata!
Down with the government!
Liberty!
Justice!
Democracy!
Respectfully,
From the mountains of southeastern Mexico,
General Command of the Clandestine Revolutionary Indigenous Committee of the EZLN.

Mexico, April 1994

◆ ◆ ◆

[This communiqué announced to the world that the EZLN would not accept the proposals negotiated by Camacho Solís and the Zapatista negotiating team in the San Cristóbal Cathedral. The use of bold type follows the original.]

Mexico, 10 June 1994

For everybody, everything. For us, nothing.
Concerning the San Cristóbal dialogue:

To the Mexican people:
To the peoples and governments of the world:

To non-governmental organizations:
To Peace Commissioner Camacho Solís:
To Bishop Samuel Ruiz:

To the national and international press:

The Clandestine Indian Revolutionary Committee-General Command of the Zapatista Liberation Army (CCRI-CG) of the Zapatista National Army of Liberation (EZLN) would like to declare the following:

1) The CCRI-CG of the EZLN has finally finished, as will be noted, the consultation with all of the towns which support it and form it. By means of assemblies in ejidos, hamlets, and outlying areas, we have learned the heartfelt desire of our supporters.

2) The CCRI-CG of the EZLN has counted the votes on the proposed peace accord offered by the federal government to the EZLN during the dialogue in San Cristóbal de las Casas, Chiapas.

3) The result of the free, democratic votes are as follows:
- In favor of the proposed peace accord: 2.11 percent.
- Against the proposed accords: 97.88 percent.

4) The vote was as follows in the simultaneous vote taken to determine the course to follow if the proposed accord is rejected:
- To resume hostilities: 3.26 percent.
- To resist and convene a new national dialogue involving all honest independent forces: 96.74 percent.

5) As a consequence of the decision of the majority of the Zapatistas, the CCRI-CG of the EZLN declares:

It rejects the proposed peace accord of the federal government.

It declares the dialogue of San Cristóbal to be over.

It calls on the people of Mexico to initiate a new national dialogue with all of the progressive forces of the country, with the central theme of democracy, liberty, and justice for all Mexicans.

The CCRI-CG of the EZLN orders regular and irregular forces in Mexico and abroad to continue the unilateral cease-fire unless they are attacked. To prevent making a political solution of the conflict even more difficult, there should be no interference in the upcoming August elections.

The EZLN pledges not to carry out any offensive military action against the federal army unless it is attacked.

The EZLN will not impede the carrying out of the elections in territory under its control and will allow the installation of polling

places under the supervision of non-governmental organizations and of the International Committee of the Red Cross.

The EZLN will not accept any aid from the federal, state, and municipal governments, and will resist the blockade with its own means and with the aid of the Mexico people.

6) The CCRI of the EZLN thanks peace negotiator Manuel Camacho Solís for his honest attempt to find a peaceful solution to the conflict. Unfortunately, the historical blindness of the central government prevented it from realizing that denying demands for democracy would lead the country to a painful confrontation, with unforeseen consequences.

7) The CCRI-CG of the EZLN would like to thank mediator Samuel Ruiz and his staff for their effort, sacrifice, and integrity, while serving as intermediaries between the parties, for his resisting pressure and threats, and for his willingness to listen. We hope to have his honest participation in the next stage of dialogue in search of a political solution to the national demands for democracy, liberty, and justice.

8) The CCRI-CG of the EZLN would like the thank the honest and independent communications media for their effort to publish the truth and let the Mexico people know what was happening, despite threats, pressure, and blackmail. We publicly ask forgiveness if, given our clumsy media policy, we harmed you or called into question your professionalism. We hope that you understand that never before have we carried out a revolution and that we are learning. We repeat that, thanks to the effort of the press, it was possible to bring the military phase of the war to a halt. We sincerely hope that you will take into consideration that the difficult conditions under which we were working contributed to our unfairly rejecting some media. We hope you continue publishing the truth.

9) The CCRI-CG of the EZLN would especially like to thank the non-governmental organizations, the vanguard of civil society, for their disinterested effort to achieve peace with justice and dignity, which is a top priority of our people. Government stone-walling now makes it difficult to reach any agreement. We continue to be open to dialogue and are ready to follow the path that you showed us with your effort—that of the political route to the transition to democracy.

10) The CCRI-CI of the EZLN salutes the men, women, children, and elderly, the anonymous ones throughout the country and aboard, for their having supported our just cause. For you, brothers and sisters, it is our struggle. For you, it will be our death. We will not rest until all Mexicans—Indians, peasants, workers, clerks, students, teachers, housewives, the urban poor, artists, honest intellectuals, the retired, the

unemployed, the marginalized, faceless men and women, without a voice—have everything they need for a dignified, fulfilling life. Everything for everybody, nothing for us.

We will continue our struggle until the Mexican flag waves over a land blessed with democracy, liberty, and justice.

Democracy!
Liberty!
Justice!

Respectfully,

Marcos

Clandestine Indigenous Revolutionary Committee-General Command of the EZLN
Mountains of Southeastern Mexico, Chiapas, Mexico June 1994.

◆ ◆ ◆

[This communiqué, dated 24 August 1994, is not from the CCRI-CG of the EZLN, but the National Democratic Convention. It remains unclear how the EZLN will juggle its relations with the Convention and with the CCRI, since it claims it will serve both.]

Declaration of the Presidency of the National Democratic Convention Concerning the Elections of 21 August 1994

After having evaluated early information on the 21 August elections, the Presidency of the National Democratic Convention reaffirms its original declaration of support for the efforts of the Mexican people to achieve a peaceful transition to democracy, to do away with the state party, and to establishing a regime based on the rule of law. This is the only possible way to resolve Mexico's grave social and economic problems. The Convention urges the documentation of electoral crimes, the cleaning up of elections, and, if appropriate, their nullification.

The elections of 21 August were exceptional in that there was heavy voter turnout, and many social and political groups from the entire nation supported the transition to democracy. However, the government preferred to maintain the state-party system, and thus organized a fraudulent election which gravely damaged the nation.

The elections of 21 August were inequitable, unjust, and fraudulent. Obviously, in a state-party regime, electoral competition is not democratic. In Mexico, inequalities are both structural and historic. There is a corrupt government, whose leaders treat it as if it were their own patrimony. It manipulates programs for political ends and uses public funds to buy votes. The legal reforms were insufficient and leave in government hands a substantial part of the preparation, organization, and judging of elections.

These events were well known before the election. The Convention and other democratic forces denounced them before election day. Despite this, and without misleading people, we urged civic participation in the election, not in support of any single candidate, but in support of the transition to democracy.

The presidency of the National Democratic Convention considers that official statistics on the election must be considered in light of extremely unequal conditions. The state party resorted to various scams, some of which would be considered criminal conduct in any election. It saturated the country with campaign literature. It prohibited alliances between opposition parties. It made unlimited use of government funds to promote the state party. That included the delivery of funds, with strings attached, by Solidarity and PROCAMPO. These funds, in many cases, were delivered the day before the election. These election crimes have been reported, but there has been practically no judicial response. There was also total control of radio and TV throughout the campaign, and especially at voting time. Various "observation" and "quick-count" groups were formed to make irrelevant, in case of controversy, the groups which the citizenry had laboriously created. This provided control over the election results. These illegitimate pressures which we Mexicans suffer are electoral crimes both morally and legally.

We must also consider the widespread irregularities that occurred on election day—vote buying, intimidation of voters, moving polling places, insufficient ballots, permitting people to vote who were not on the voter list or who were registered at distant polling places. Absentee voters could not vote in special polling places established for them, since early voting by police and military men at these polling places used up all the ballots. There were also flying squads voting repeatedly, as well as the busing in of voters.

At some polling places, people were allowed to vote without an ID. In other cases, the indelible ink approved by the Federal Electoral Institute was not used. Voters were intimidated on election day. There was old-style fraud, which official sources claimed had disappeared. Examples included the theft of ballot boxes, forced votes in Indian areas, and the setting up of safe houses where fake ballots were filled out. The fraudulent practices varied from place to place.

The Convention has received very detailed information indicating that there was also computer fraud, which caused the delay in publishing results from 10 percent of the polling places. According to an audit, 17 percent of the citizens did not appear on their voter list. This indicates the deliberate shifting of names to lists at other polling places to confuse voters. In 32 percent of the polling places, multiple voting was permitted. In 65 percent, voters were deleted from the voter list, and in at least a quarter of polling places, voting was not secret.

Preliminary official results of the presidential elections should be interpreted in light of various factors. If indeed the PRI received more than 40 percent of the vote, and the PAN received more than 20 percent, and the PRD below 20 percent, it would be an error to think that that accurately expressed the political will of the Mexican people.

The Presidency of the National Democratic Convention considers that most of the votes for the PRI can be explained by these illegalities and by deliberate manipulation of the mass media, which created the expectation that political change would result in widespread violence and disorder. Thus, we do not feel the vote for the PRI should be interpreted as support for the neo-liberal policies that have divided the nation into a deprived, manipulated, impoverished majority and a handful of multi-millionaire businessmen.

The elections, as we all know, took place under a state-party system. There was inequality between parties. However, on the twenty-first, other facts became apparent. Despite the political system and voter manipulation, more than half of the voters voted against the PRI. Given existing political conditions, this represents an enormous vote of censure for the government. It also indicates that there is a social base that potentially could struggle for a democratic transition.

Many attempted to vote, but there was no corresponding increase in voter turnout. Millions of Mexicans could not vote since they were left off the voter list. In 1994, apparently there were more citizens who voted for the PRI, but there were also more citizens who voted against the PRI. This was a clear majority which even fraud could not cover up. Widespread evidence indicates that the PRI vote reflected not only those who approved of official policy, but the old corporate vote, votes which were bought, votes based on public and private deals cut with the Zedillo campaign, and votes based on fear, induced by official declarations which linked political change to disorder and violence. And of course some votes were fabricated in "safe houses" and by key strokes on computation center computers.

The PAN vote, in contrast, almost doubled in both relative and absolute terms. The number of votes for Cárdenas does not reflect his demonstrated ability to organize and draw crowds. His vote reflects a five-year-long official campaign of attacks as well as massive manipulation before and after 21 August. Cárdenas' supporters form a broad social movement for democracy and a broad civic alliance promoting peace, democracy, and social justice.

Those who benefit from elections see them as closing the book on the old order, continuity, undemocratic practices, and neo-liberal injustices. For us, they are another battle in the long struggle for democracy and justice. This battle not only showed the increasing weakness and desperation of the system, but its inertia and political resources. It was also a battle which showed the strength and militancy of the civic movement for democracy. Finally, it shows insufficient penetration among the discontented, but confused and terrorized, majority.

The National Democratic Convention, since its founding in Augascalientes, Chiapas, has called on citizens to vote and to monitor elections. After evaluating the fraud, it calls citizens to defend election honesty and to struggle by legal means to prevent the continued violation of popular will. We invite all those who have evidence of fraudulent practices to report them to their state representatives. It also calls on State Conventions to organize forums for analysis. Those "shaved" from voting lists should be strongly encouraged to attend.

The Convention once again demonstrates its commitment to peace in Chiapas and its decision to prevent any attacks on the EZLN. It also wants to create the political environment in which the legitimate demands of Indians and peasants can be pursued by peaceful means and with constitutional guarantees. The elections of 21 August and the present citizens' insurgency are not the last battle, but only one stage of a long struggle.

After considering the official results of the election in Chiapas, the data from the citizen's movement, and the multiple irregularities which have been documented, the National Democratic Convention (CND) strongly supports the victory claim of civil society and of the PRD, led by their candidate Amado Avendaño. The CND supports the mobilization of the Chiapan people to prevent the imposition of an illegitimate governor.

The Convention presidency calls on all Mexicans to protest next Saturday, the twenty-seventh, at noon in the plazas of their towns and cities. The demonstration will protest election fraud and the state party. Also, it will support democratic transition and the struggle of the Chiapan people.

It convokes all convention members to a "Democracy Day," Sunday, 4 September, at 10 a.m.

Once the election has been certified, the Convention will consult with other civic organizations concerning the establishment of a People's Electoral Tribunal, which will rule on the validity of the 1994 election.

Thus, the Convention demands clean elections or their annulment if they do not meet the criteria established by the Constitution.

The Convention has taken up as it own the EZLN's demands for democracy. As a result, we support its firm decision for peace. Thus, it rejects imposition and supports the political transformation that is needed.

The civil society is assuming responsibility and will not yield in its demand that Mexico be democratized by peaceful means.

The National Democratic Convention considers that it is necessary to establish a legitimate, pluralistic, representative government in Mexico. It should be based on the rule of law, with a broad democratic transition program. As part of the reform, a constitutional congress could be called and democratic elections could be held for the first time in Mexican history.

This election was a crucial stage in the long road to democracy in Mexico. There has been unprecedented citizen participation throughout the intense campaigns, during the poll watching, and now with the reports of irregularities and with the struggle to clean up elections. This mobilized force serves as a solid base for a new democratic movement. Its invaluable experiences will serve the civil struggles. This force and this knowledge should be preserved and increased.

Within a few days, the presidency of the National Convention will convene a second session. In a spirit of unity, it convokes all of the citizens of Mexico, and the diverse social and political forces, to join a new effort to defend democracy.

The presidency of the National Democratic Convention shares the indignation of the Mexican people at the fraud and exhorts everyone to keep elections honest and defend their rights in a legal manner so as to achieve peace with justice and dignity.

Mexico City, 24 August 1994

Rosario Ibarra: President
Luis Javier Garrido: Vice president
José Álvarez Icaza: Vice president
Antonio Hernández: Vice president
Mariclarie Acosta: Secretary

Appendix III: Keeping Current

Mexico Resource Center
Box 7547
Austin, TX 78713
Tel. 512/458-4518

Beginning in January 1995, the Mexico Resource Center will publish a cumulative, monthly supplement to *The Chiapas Rebellion.*

Documentation Exchange
Box 2327
Austin, TX 78768
Tel. 512/476-9841

The Documentation Exchange publishes the biweekly *Mexico NewsPac,* a compilation of newspaper articles on Chiapas and other Mexico-related themes.

Global Exchange
2017 Mission St., Rm. 303
San Francisco, CA 94116
Tel. 415/255-7296

Global Exchange offers a variety of publications on Chiapas.

National Commission for Democracy in Mexico, USA
601 Cotton St., Suite A 103
El Paso, Tx 79902
Tel. 915/565-5970

The Commission has been commissioned by the EZLN to supply information on Chiapas in the United States.

Grassroots International
48 Grove St., No. 103
Somerville, MA 02144
Tel. 617/628-1664

Grassroots International publishes reports on human-rights abuse in Mexico.

Bibliography:

Academia Mexicana de Derechos Humanos (1987) *Chiapas: cronología de un etnocidio reciente.* Mexico City.

Amnesty International (1986) *Mexico: Human Rights in Rural Areas, Exchange of Documents with the Mexican Government on Human Rights Violations in Oaxaca and Chiapas.* London.

— (1994) *Amnesty International Delegation in Mexico Confirms Reports of Human Rights Violations during Chiapas Uprising.* AI Index: 41/WU 03/1994.

Bailón, Moisés J. (1994) "Semejanzas y diferencias en dos regiones indígenas del sur de México; Oaxaca y Chiapas a la luz de la revuelta del EZLN." Paper presented at the XVIII Congress of the Latin American Studies Association, Atlanta.

Baitenmann, Helga (1994) "'Lo que no procede': the Reforms to Article 27 and the Coffee Sector in Central Veracruz." Paper presented at the XVIII Congress of the Latin American Studies Association, Atlanta.

Barberán, José, Cuauhtémoc Cárdenas, Adriana López Monjardin & Jorge Zavala (1988) *Radiografía del fraude.* Mexico City: Nuestro Tiempo.

Bardach, Ann Louise (1994) "Mexico's Poet Rebel," *Vanity Fair* 57 (July): 68-74, 130-35.

Bartra, Armando (1994) "Chiapas en el centro," *La Jornada del Campo* 39 (6 Sept.): 1-3.

Benjamin, Thomas (1989) *A Rich Land, A Poor People: Politics and Society in Modern Chiapas.* Albuquerque: University of New Mexico Press.

Bolívar, Augusto & Luiz Méndez (1994a) "Entre el consenso pasivo y la crítica de las armas," *El Cotidiano* 61 (March-April): 68-81.

— (1994b) "La hora de las definiciones pendientes: jornadas para la paz y la reconciliación en Chiapas," *El Cotidiano* 63 (July-Aug.): 64-70.

Burbach, Roger (1994) "Roots of the Postmodern Rebellion in Chiapas," *New Left Review* 205 (May-June): 113-24.

Camú Urzúa, Guido & Dauno Tótoro Taulis (1994) *EZLN: El Ejército que salió de la selva.* Mexico City: Planeta.

Cancian, Frank & Peter Brown (1994) "Who is Rebelling in Chiapas?" *Cultural Survival Quarterly* 18 (Spring): 22-25.

Casas, Yoloxóchitl & Laura Castellanos (1994) "Causas de la marginación política de las mujeres chiapanecas," *Fem* 134 (April): 16.

Cleaver, Harry (1994) "Introduction, " pp. 11-23, *¡Zapatistas! Documents of the New Mexican Revolution.* Brooklyn: Autonomedia.

Collier, George A. (1994) "Roots of the Rebellion in Chiapas," *Cultural Survival Quarterly* 18 (Spring): 14-18.

Comisión Mexicana de Defensa y Promoción de los Derechos Humanos, Centro Miguel Agustín Pro & Centro Fray Francisco de Vitoria (1994) *Informe preliminar a la Comisión Interamericana de Derechos Humanos.* Mexico City.

Conger, Lucy (1994) "Zapatista Thunder," *Current History* 93 (March): 115-20.

De Vos, Jan (1992) *Los enredos de remesal: ensayo sobre la conquista de Chiapas.* Mexico City: Consejo Nacional para la Cultura y las Artes.

Del Muro, Ricardo (1994) "Movimientos campesinos: la violenta lucha por la tierra," *Macrópolis* 98 (31 Jan.): 16-23.

Díaz-Polanco, Héctor (1994) "Autonomía y racismo," *CEMOS Memoria* 63 (Feb.): 17-20.

Editorial Collective (1994) *¡Zapatistas! Documents of the New Mexican Revolution.* Brooklyn: Autonomedia.

García de León, Antonio (1985) *Resistencia y utopía* (2 vols.). Mexico City: Era.

Gijsbers, Wim (1994) "Simojovel," *Ojarasca* 33-34 (June-July): 21-24.

Gómez, Arturo Santamaría (1994) "Zapatistas Deliver a Message from 'Deep Mexico,'" *Z Magazine* (March): 30-33.

Gosner, Kevin (1992) *Soldiers of the Virgin: the Moral Economy of a Colonial Maya Rebellion.* Tucson: University of Arizona Press.

Gossen, Gary H. (1994) "Comments on the Zapatista Movement," *Cultural Survival Quarterly* 18 (Spring): 19-21.

Guillermoprieto, Alma (1994) "Zapata's Heirs," *New Yorker* 70 (16 May): 52-63.

Harvey, Neil (1994a) "Las lecciones de Chiapas," *Ojarasca* 37 (Oct.): 6-10.

— (1994b) "Rebellion in Chiapas: Rural Reforms, Campesino Radicalism, and the Limits to Salinismo," pp. 1-43, *Transformation of Rural Mexico*, Number 5. Center for U.S.-Mexican Studies, University of California at San Diego.

Hernández Castillo, Rosalva Aída (1992) "Los refugios guatemaltecos y la dinámica fronteriza en Chiapas," pp. 93-105, *Una década de refugio en México*, ed. Graciela Freyermuth Enciso. Mexico City: Centro de Investigaciones y Estudios Superiores en Antropología Social & Instituto Chiapaneco de Cultura & Academia Mexicana de Derechos Humanos.

— (1994) "La 'fuerza extraña' es mujer," *Ojarasca* 30 (March): 36-37.

Hernández Navarro, Luis (1994a) "The Chiapas Uprising," pp. 44-56, *Transformation of Rural Mexico*, Number 5. Center for U.S.-Mexican Studies, University of California at San Diego.

— (1994b) "Por la ruta de los fierros," *Cuadernos de Nexos* 68 (Feb.): xxiv-xxvi.

— (1994c) "Chiapas: restructuración y cambio," *El Cotidiano* 61 (March-April) 4-11.

— (1994d) "The New Mayan War," *NACLA Report on the Americas* 27 (March-April): 6-10.

— (1994e) "Chiapas: la marea campesina," *La Jornada del Campo* 30 (4 Oct.): 1-3.

Huchim, Eduardo (1994) *México 1994: la rebelión y el magnicidio.* Mexico City: Nueva Imagen.

Human Rights Watch/Americas (1994) *Mexico: The New Year's Rebellion.* New York.

Knight, Alan (1994) "Chiapas: Myths and Misconceptions," *El Financiero Internacional* 3 (7 Feb.): 6.

Lagunes, Lucía (1994) "Nosotras en la Convención," 140 *Fem* (Oct.): 24-25.

Medina, Andrés (1994) "Autonomía y derechos de los pueblos indios," CEM*OS Memoria* 65 (April): 12-15.

Méndez Asensio, Luis & Antonio Cano Gimeno (1994) *La guerra contra el tiempo.* Mexico City: Ediciones Temas de Hoy.

Minnesota Advocates for Human Rights (1992) *Conquest Continued: Disregard for Human and Indigenous Rights in the Mexican State of Chiapas.* Minneapolis.

Moguel, Julio (1994) "El Pronasol en el horno chiapaneco," *El Cotidiano* 61 (March-April): 12-20.

Morín, José Luis (1994) "An Indigenous People's Struggle for Justice," *Covert Action* 48 (Spring): 38-43.

Morris, Vincent (1994) "Rainforest Revolt," *Audubon* 96 (May-June): 16-18.

Nigh, Ronald (1994) "Zapata Rose in 1994," *Cultural Survival Quarterly* 18 (Spring): 9-13.

Pazos, Luis (1994) *¿Por qué Chiapas?* Mexico City: Diana.

Piñeyro, José Luis (1994) "Los por qué de la corta guerra en Chiapas," *El Cotidiano* 63 (July-Aug.): 3-7.

Reding, Andrew (1994) "Chiapas Is Mexico: The Imperative of Political Reform," *World Policy Journal* 11 (Spring): 11-25.

Reygadas, Pedro, Iván Gómezcesar & Esther Kravzov (eds.) (1994) *La guerra de Año Nuevo.* Mexico City: Praxis.

Riding, Alan (1985) *Distant Neighbors.* New York: Knopf.

Rodríguez, Erwin (1987) "La frontera Sur: notas sobre la repetina interrupción de un sueño," pp. 297-321, *17 ángulos de un sexenio.* Mexico City: Plaza y Valdés.

Romero Jacobo, César (1994a) *Los Altos de Chiapas.* Mexico City: Planeta.

— (1994b) *Marcos: ¿Un profesional de la esperanza?* Mexico City: Planeta.

Ross, John (1994) *Rebellion from the Roots.* Monroe, Maine: Common Courage.

Russell, Philip (1994) *Mexico under Salinas.* Austin: Mexico Resource Center.

Tamayo Flores-Alatorre, Sergio (1994) "Origen y novedad en el EZLN," *La Jornada Semanal* 245 (20 Feb.): 39-43.

Toledo, Víctor M. (1994) "El mito del indígena ignorante (y su aplicación al caso de Chiapas)," *Ojarasca* 30 (March): 6-12.

Tovar Nieves, Yolanda (1994) "Los vilipendiados derechos humanos en el conflicto chiapaneco," *El Cotidiano* 63 (July-Aug.): 89-96.

Trejo Delarbre, Raúl (1994) *Chiapas: La comunicación enmascarada.* Mexico City: Diana.

Urbina Nandayapa, Arturo de Jesús (1994) *Las razones de Chiapas.* Mexico City: Editorial PAC

Vázquez Aguirre, David (1994) "Algunas causas que explican el levantamiento armado en Chiapas," *El Cotidiano* 61 (March-April): 26-31.

Weinberg, Bill (1994) "¡Viva Zapata! Revolution Rocks Southern Mexico," *High Times* 228 (Aug.): 18-21, 56-57.

Zea, Leopoldo (1994) "Chiapas, yunque de México para Latinoamérica," *Cuadernos Americanos* 43 (Jan.-Feb.): 11-42.

Index